How to Go to College on a Shoe String

The Insider's Guide
to Grants, Scholarships,
Cheap Books, Fellowships and
Other Financial Aid Secrets

~ 2nd Edition ~

By Ann Marie O'Phelan

Revised By: Debra Lipphardt

How to Go to College on a Shoe String:
The Insider's Guide to Grants, Scholarships, Cheap Books, Fellowships and Other Financial Aid Secrets - 2nd Edition

Copyright © 2016 Atlantic Publishing Group, Inc.
1405 SW 6th Avenue • Ocala, Florida 34471 • Phone 800-814-1132 • Fax 352-622-1875
Website: www.atlantic-pub.com • Email: sales@atlantic-pub.com
SAN Number: 268-1250

Library of Congress Cataloging-in-Publication Data

Names: Lipphardt, Debra, 1954- author. | O'Phelan, Ann Marie, 1960- previous
   edition. How to go to college on a shoe string,
Title: How to go to college on a shoe string : the insider's guide to grants,
   scholarships, cheap books, fellowships and other financial aid secrets /
   Debra Lipphardt.
Description: Revised 2nd edition. | Ocala, Fla. : Atlantic Publishing Group,
   Inc., 2016. | Revised edition of: How to go to college on a shoe string /
   Ann Marie O'Phelan. | Includes bibliographical references and index.
Identifiers: LCCN 2015050644| ISBN 9781620231180 (alk. paper) | ISBN
   1620231182 (alk. paper)
Subjects: LCSH: Student aid--United States--Handbooks, manuals, etc. |
   College costs--United States--Handbooks, manuals, etc.
Classification: LCC LB2337.4 .O64 2016 | DDC 378.3/8--dc23 LC record
available at http://lccn.loc.gov/2015050644

Printed in the United States

EDITOR: Rebekah Sack • rsack@atlantic-pub.com
INTERIOR LAYOUT AND JACKET DESIGN: Antoinette D'Amore • addesign@videotron.ca
COVER DESIGN: Meg Buchner • meg@megbuchner.com

Printed on Recycled Paper

Reduce. Reuse. RECYCLE.

A decade ago, Atlantic Publishing signed the Green Press Initiative. These guidelines promote environmentally friendly practices, such as using recycled stock and vegetable-based inks, avoiding waste, choosing energy-efficient resources, and promoting a no-pulping policy. We now use 100-percent recycled stock on all our books. The results: in one year, switching to post-consumer recycled stock saved 24 mature trees, 5,000 gallons of water, the equivalent of the total energy used for one home in a year, and the equivalent of the greenhouse gases from one car driven for a year.

Over the years, we have adopted a number of dogs from rescues and shelters. First there was Bear and after he passed, Ginger and Scout. Now, we have Kira, another rescue. They have brought immense joy and love not just into our lives, but into the lives of all who met them.

We want you to know a portion of the profits of this book will be donated in Bear, Ginger and Scout's memory to local animal shelters, parks, conservation organizations, and other individuals and nonprofit organizations in need of assistance.

– Douglas & Sherri Brown,
President & Vice-President of Atlantic Publishing

Table of Contents

Preface

y now, we all know that the cost of getting an education is soaring. College Board, a not-for-profit membership association whose mission is to connect students to college success and opportunities, states in their report "Tuition and Fees and Room and Board Over Time":

> Average published tuition and fees in the public four-year sector rose by 2.8%, 2.9%, and 2.9% in 2013-14, 2014-15, and 2015-16, respectively, the smallest current dollar increases since the mid-1970s. The inflation-adjusted increases were 0.8% in 2013-14, 0.9% in 2014-15, and 2.7% in 2015-16.
> **(https://trends.collegeboard.org)**

These days, getting a college degree is vital to working in many fields, including nursing, teaching, and engineering. But even with the hefty price tag, getting an education makes good economic sense. According to the most recent College Board "Education Pays" report, authored by Sandy Baum, Jennifer Ma, and Kathleen Payea, those with bachelor's degrees will earn roughly $21,100 more than those with high school diplomas only. Another fun fact from the report: "The median four-year college graduate who enrolls at age 18 and graduates in four years can expect to earn enough by age 36 to compensate for being out of the labor force for four years, as well as for borrowing the full amount required to pay tuition and feed without any grant assistance."

That all sounds great, but at the end of the day, you have to figure out how to get the money for college. Yes, tuition and costs are rising, but there is good news: According to the most recent College Board "Trends in Student Aid" report, $236.7 billion in financial aid was distributed to undergraduate and graduate students for the 2011-12 school year. There are low-interest loans, grants, scholarships, cooperative education, work-study programs, and more, all designed to help you get that degree.

So where do you start? The first thing you should do is apply for all the free college money that you can. Grants and scholarships can help, and their values can range from as low as $250 to assisting with covering the entire cost of college. Yes, the entire four years can sometimes be paid in full by a grant, but not for most of us. Once the free money sources are exhausted, you should check out student loans. Student loans can provide you with low-interest rates, and you will not have to worry about starting payments until six months after you graduate. They can even defer payment an additional two or three months for special circumstances. That gives you plenty of time to find a job in your chosen profession and be in a position to make payments. Even if you are able to make loan payments, it is in your best interest to make them as low as possible. There are also other resources for money, such as home-equity loans, private loans, and retirement fund loans. But those should be considered only after you have exercised your other options, and you should seek the advice of a financial adviser before even thinking about it.

How to Go to College on a Shoe String: The Insider's Guide to Grants, Scholarships, Cheap Books, Fellowships, and Other Financial Aid Secrets is designed to help you find out what college funds are available to help you pursue your education and how to get through college as inexpensively as possible from your first day of school until graduation. Chapter by chapter, you can explore what money and opportunities are available and how to apply for and receive the funds for your education — whether you are working on a certification program, two-year degree, a four-year degree, a master's degree, or even a doctorate degree. Plus, you will learn all sorts of tips and helpful information to stretch the dollars that you do have.

Cutting college costs wherever possible will result in that much less for you to pay back once you finish your education. And once the "normal, real-life" bills start rolling in, like the mortgage, the car payment, and the insurance, you will be glad you did everything you could to take advantage of college funds that were designed to help students like yourself pursue their education more affordably.

Introduction

hile there are a lot of books out there designed to help you cut back on your education costs, this book is one of the more comprehensive books on the market, and one of the easiest to follow. From providing you with the contact information for grants, scholarships, and loans to explaining all the steps you need to take to apply for and win them, this book will guide you through the process of finding money for college from start to finish. Additionally, you will pick up some great money-saving tips along the way.

How to Read This Book

There is a wealth of information in this book, but to get the maximum value out of it, you need to read it from cover to cover. If you are short on time and attention, you can always read the chapters you are most interested in first.

For instance, if you are one of the one million students who have been home-schooled and you are wondering how that affects your college application, you will find helpful information in Chapter 1. Although home-schooled students enjoy a reputation as being well-prepared for college and tend to score better on the SATs and other standardized tests than regular students, colleges sometimes expect your home-schooling to be well-documented, which you can read more about in Chapter 1.

If you are wondering about the application process and what kinds of forms you generally need to fill out and what paperwork you need to provide schools with, Chapter 2 will outline what to expect, from getting your transcripts to gathering letters of recommendation to preparing for your interview.

Say you have heard about the Free Application for Federal Student Aid (FAFSA), but you are not sure what it is. Chapter 3 spells it out for you and tells you how to apply. The FAFSA is a form that schools, government agencies, and many scholarship committees use to generate the Student Aid Report (SAR) to determine your financial need. This report determines how much money (free or loans) you are going to get for college.

Maybe you have already received a scholarship, but it did not cover enough of your costs. What do you do? Chapters 4 and 5 cover grants and loans that may offer the perfect supplement to your scholarship. Everything is covered in these two chapters to help you find the funding that is right for you — from specifics on how to apply for the funding to who is qualified to receive the funds.

Perhaps you have heard about cooperative education (education that blends academics with hands-on work) but you were not quite sure what it is. Chapter 6 will explain it and give you information on how to pursue it so you can zero in on cutting college costs while gaining work experience to help build your résumé.

If you have attempted to navigate the scholarship jungle, then you must know that it can be complex and daunting. Chapters 7 and 8 concentrate on answering all of your scholarship questions, while providing helpful information on how to pursue scholarship funds — everything you need is included, from writing an effective essay to where to look for those scholarship dollars.

Of course, there are scams out there designed to rip you off under the guise of helping you receive college funds. Chapter 9 outlines what to watch out for so you are less likely to be taken advantage of by unscrupulous companies or private individuals looking to steal your identity or your money.

You may have received plenty of college funding from student loans, grants, and scholarships, but you still need to keep your spending under control. Chapter 10 is filled with helpful tips and ideas on how to cut personal spending and save a few dollars along the way.

Whether you are a freshman studying political science, a sophomore pursuing a teaching degree, a junior on your way to becoming a marine biologist, or a senior studying pre-law, you will find all the information you need to get the money that is available for you to finish your education, and you will also find out the best way to put those dollars to work.

While the cost of getting an education is soaring, more money is available for students than ever before. Once you finish reading this book, you will know where to find that money and how to go about getting it more effectively. You can zero in on the chapters that apply most to you or dive in and read the entire book. Either way, you should learn a great deal.

What to Do Once You Finish This Book

You can read about getting education funding until you are blue in the face, but it will not do any good unless you take the necessary steps to apply for the money. Getting funds of any sort — from loans to grants to scholarships — takes some effort on your part. You may have to fill out an application, apply for FAFSA, write an essay, or prove that you have financial need. It may take you hours or days to prepare, depending on what it is you are applying for, but by cutting costs you are essentially paying yourself. Once the student grants and scholarships come in, all of that time will be worthwhile.

Chapter 1

How Am I Going to Pay for College?

Higher education has never been cheap, but costs have skyrocketed in recent years. According to the College Board, tuition increases have outpaced the cost of living for the last 20 years. From the 2006-2007 college year to 2014-2015, college tuition and fees have more than doubled. The cost of food, books, housing, transportation, and other expenses have also risen. The good news is that with some research and effort you can bring your college expenses down to an affordable level or even have them paid for completely.

Once you have the money you need for college and know how to spend it wisely to stretch every dollar to the max, you are ready. But before all of this can begin, you need to start with the basics. First, which college are you going to attend?

It is never too early to start preparing for college. To maximize your scholarship potential, you should not only keep your grades up but also participate in a variety of extracurricular activities and community service so that when the time comes to fill out applications, you will shine. There are also inexpensive ways of knocking out course credits while still in high school. Advanced Placement courses, the International Baccalaureate Program (IB), the Advanced International Certificate of Education (AICE), CLEP exams, and completing coursework at a local community college can reduce the time and costs you will need to spend at an expensive college while also preparing you for college courses. Since your time is limited, you need to weigh these options carefully to ensure that you finish high school with a well-balanced record. You could even be on you way to finishing your freshman year before you even leave home. Although your schedule may be full, if you have a goal in mind and work steadily toward it, the end results will be well worth it.

CASE STUDY:
PHYLLIS REARDON,
Life Coach

As a life coach, I help people discover what they want in life and set goals to achieve success. The following helpful hints have been modified from my Goal Setting Workshop for Parents.

As you prepare to enter college, a new journey in your life, achieving success will be determined by how well you plan.

Goal Setting

Success in college takes planning, and a big part of planning is setting goals. Goal setting is asking the question: What do I want from college? Once you know your goals, the next step is designing strategies or actions. Success comes when you reach the goals or outcomes you set.

Goal Setting Activity

Writing a term paper:

First, create a schedule and break up the work in doable-sized pieces. Display this schedule on your wall, desk, or day planner as a daily visual reminder. Schedule the day of the week and exact time to work on the paper. Make a note of the grade you want to receive. Announce to family or friends when the paper will be complete. Making your goal public can help create motivation for completion as it sets up monitors. There are 168 hours in a week — use them wisely. Goals need strategies. Strategies define actions. Action leads to success.

Your Future View

Did you know that the more clearly defined a picture you have of yourself in the future the more likely you are to reach it? This picture of yourself could be called your possible self, the person you want to be. But pictures are not enough. Goals must be set and actions taken to be successful.

> ***Your Future View Activity***
> Create a picture of yourself by asking where you want to be in five years. What does it look like? What diploma or degree is hanging on your wall? Where are you working? Where are you living? What is your salary? What car are you driving? Now make a list of the necessary actions steps to reach this desired self.

College Knowledge

New experiences like entering college may cause feelings of uncertainty, worry, and even fear. One way to lessen these real concerns is to become well-informed. Knowledge is power. Increase your power. Correct information always seems to dispel doubts, so research your college. Know what the rules and regulations are, check out your course descriptions and determine what is expected of you, check out tuition payments, campus recreation/social clubs, even parking permits. Know how the library system works. Know who to contact if faced with unforeseen obstacles. Check out adviser/mentor or buddy programs, help centers, and the student council.

Take control, search the web, plan, and increase your college knowledge.

Success will happen, but only if you plan.

Whose Job Is This?

Getting ready for college, if done right, is an ongoing process that can last throughout your high school years. The workload increases tremendously your senior year as you begin narrowing choices for schools, start completing application packets, and continue working on financial aid. Hundreds of choices have to be made, big and small. The biggest are the choice of college and major, but there are countless decisions to be made about the details of financial aid, where you are going to live, and how all of this is going to be paid for. These decisions can create lots of stress for families as students try to assert their independence and parents try to retain control and do what they think is best. Your college process can go down in flames if you and your parents are at odds about everything from which college to attend to who is responsible for licking the stamps.

This needs to be a team effort, with rights and responsibilities for both parties. You need to sit down together early in the process and spell out what each side expects of the other. Open communication is the key to getting through this. The family relationship is changing, and as this process rolls along, parents can watch their child evolve into adulthood. Here are some points to keep in mind to make this transition a smoother one.

- Ultimately, the choice of school and major should rest with you — the student. It is your life, and you are the one who is going to have to live with the consequences. Your parents' job is to offer advice and counsel. However, you have to consider their point of view. You need to remember that your parents have been out in the real world for many years, and they really do know more about making a living and the working world. Plus, if they are helping you pay, they may want to have more of a say in what you choose to study. For instance, they may help pay for a degree in graphic design but not sculpture. Or they help pay for an in-state public school but not an out-of-state or private one. Or if they are footing the entire bill, it may be their way or no way.

- Your parents should help handle the financial aid forms. Parents have experience and knowledge about finances that you do not have. However, this is a great opportunity for your parents to work together with you and teach you how money works. Some parents might feel uneasy laying bare their financial picture, particularly if they have spent your college fund on cruises to the Bahamas, but keep in mind that you are about to go off on your own and are more likely to do well if you begin to understand how family finances operate.

- Beginning in your senior year, if not before, you and your parents are going to start accumulating forms and documents for college admissions, scholarships, and financial aid. These responsibilities can be divided. For example, you could be responsible for admissions and scholarship forms, but your parents could assume the role of supervisor and make sure everything is on track and deadlines are met.

- Even if you win a lot of financial aid, there may be unmet costs. Make it clear who is going to pick up the tab, and for what amount. Do your parents expect you to get a part-time job while in school to take care of daily expenses, or are they willing or able to provide an allowance? Are you going to take care of clothing and automobile expenses, or are your parents? Who is going to pay for the plane tickets at Thanksgiving and Christmas if your college is far from home? Are you going to have to live at home and commute to a nearby college?

- Make it clear who is responsible for paying off those college loans that you are more than likely going to have to incur. Since you are going to benefit from a college education in terms of a higher salary, you should be the one to pay off the loan. However, some parents want their child to start out in life debt-free, and they have the means to take on this burden. If this is the case, your parents should consider withholding this offer until graduation. It might be sneaky, but if you feel that you have a big financial stake in doing well and landing a good job, you are likely to work harder and be more responsible about the choices you make in school. Whichever way your family decides to go, make sure everyone knows from the outset who is responsible.

By sharing the load, you can keep peace and harmony in your household throughout this process. When the stress level rises, and deadlines are looming, and it all seems overwhelming, everyone should keep in mind that the ultimate goal is to get you the best possible start in life. It is all going to be worth it.

Going It Alone

The whole financial aid process assumes that parents are helping you along every step of the way and that they are going to foot a large portion of the bill. Of course, this is not the case for many. Students come from every conceivable financial situation, and the aid process is not equipped to deal with all of them. Some parents refuse to help, some parents are financially unable to help, and some parents are in jail or hanging out at a Tibetan monastery finding themselves. If you are in one of these situations or something similar, you are on your own. Unfortunately, the financial aid process may not see it that way.

As far as financial aid is concerned, you can declare yourself to be an independent student if you are at least 24 years old by Dec. 31 of the award year, and the only other ways to declare independence are if you are married as of the date you file for financial aid, a military veteran, an orphan or ward of the court, if you have a child for whom you provide at least 50 percent support (and you have to have proof that you are doing that), or if you are emancipated from your parents or homeless.

The financial aid office at your college also has the authority to declare you an independent student, but you are going to have to demonstrate very unusual circumstances. If your parents are both in jail, hospitalized, institutionalized, or if they have just plain abandoned you for some reason, be prepared to document this circumstance and produce reliable witnesses on your behalf, such as a clergy member or social worker, or possibly through some high school personnel if necessary. Being an independent student generally makes you eligible for more aid since only your income is being counted toward your ability to pay. However, individual schools may have tougher criteria for independence than the federal government because it is in their interest not to grant this status. Even if you are declared to be an independent student, some colleges require that parents complete the FAFSA anyway and still may use their incomes.

What if your parents have money, are not in jail or a mental institution, but still refuse to contribute one dime toward your college education? This situation is rare, but it does happen. Some parents believe that their children should make their own way in this world, which includes making it through college without any financial support from them. This might build your character, but the bad news is that the financial aid office is going to act as if your parents are contributing, and you are not going to get an extra dime. Also, in reality, many families fall under the "middle class" status; where they make too much to get any assistance besides the minimal loans yet cannot afford to help you. In either case, you are going to have to find other ways to fund your education.

What You Can Do to Get Ready

You are already doing the most important thing you need to do to get ready for college, which is learning all you can about the right decisions to make. Getting the most out of financial aid opportunities and making the right choices requires arming yourself with information and getting a good plan together. You can change your plan as your needs change, but the important thing is that you keep moving toward your goal of getting the best college education as cheaply as possible.

There are many sources of information available. College catalogs and their online websites contain a wealth of information about their schools. Pay special attention to costs and financial aid requirements and deadlines. School websites contain a wealth of material about scholarships, academic programs, extracurricular activities, and campus life. Websites are becoming more informative, although they can sometimes be rather difficult to navigate to find all you need to know. And with some smaller colleges, they may be behind with their websites and it might be just a condensed version of their catalog, which has more important details. But as time and technology move on, many colleges rely on the internet to impart their information and no longer mail their catalogs or brochures unless requested. When you finally find the few colleges that you are sincerely interested in, search their website thoroughly and, if possible, request a catalog.

The internet offers a gateway to loads of helpful information, from SAT/ACT prep courses to little-known private scholarship opportunities. The Appendix contains a list of helpful sites, and you should take a look at all of them.

You also need to get organized early on. Keep a notebook to start jotting down notes about helpful information that you might want to review later. Make a folder, either a hard copy or on your computer, to store any letters of recommendation, awards you have received, or any college-worthy essays. Get a calendar to keep track of admissions and scholarship deadlines and important financial aid dates. You are going to be keeping track of a hundred things at once, and you don't want to miss financial aid or scholarship opportunities because you turned in an application too late.

Make sure you keep copies of financial aid forms and applications (another use for your folder). If you are applying for numerous scholarships, having copies of work you have already done can save you valuable time and energy, and it can help you keep track of what you have completed so far. If you have an interview to go on for one of the scholarships, reviewing the application will be helpful. Also, there is always the possibility that a valuable form can get lost in the mail, the fax can fail to arrive, or the email disappears into cyberspace. Do not be afraid to pick up the phone and make sure an important application has arrived. These disasters may not happen very often, but this is too important a process to leave to chance.

Once you have educated yourself about the opportunities that are out there, start putting a plan together that will help you achieve your goals. Start thinking about scholarship requirements and how you are going to meet them. Also, you should start thinking about the best ways for you to knock out course credits early.

Savings Plans

Putting money aside for a child's education, if possible, is a great idea for parents. Many states now have savings plans offering tax benefits that carry on even while a child is attending college. Savings will reduce the amount of financial aid you are going to need and, most importantly, the amount of money that you may have to borrow.

There is a tricky relationship, however, between savings and financial aid. A mistaken belief is that savings is going to reduce the amount of aid you can receive, so you are better off spending the money and pinning your hopes on a big aid check. For example, if you and your parents have saved enough to pay for your entire college education, you are not going to receive the amount of aid you would have received if you had no savings at all. However, only a fraction of it is counted toward the expected family contribution. The financial aid process does not expect parents to put their entire life savings toward a college education for their children. What this means is that you can have enough money in the bank to pay for college, and you might still be eligible for financial aid. You are better off with money in the bank that is earning interest for you and providing tax benefits than without any money at all.

However, it is a bad idea to save money in your own name. This will have a big impact on the amount of financial aid that you can receive because it is counted among your assets and it is assumed that all of this money can go toward college expenses.

Any amount of savings is going to help, but the best and most practical plan is to start early and be consistent. For example, if you save $25 per week until your child is 17 years old and your annual rate of return is five percent, you will save $35,272. If parents start saving when the child is older, they will have to make a bigger contribution to get that kind of payoff, but any amount that can be set aside for the future will pay dividends.

There are several ways to save money. You can simply place money in a regular savings account at a bank, but you probably are going to earn a low interest rate, and you will have to pay federal and state income taxes on what you do earn.

A better place to stash your college fund is a Section 529 plan. These plans are administered by states so the rules and regulations vary from state to state. The money that is placed into these plans is tax-deferred, like IRA or 401(k) contributions, but the bonus is that qualified disbursements are not taxed either. This allows parents to get the most bang for their buck. Even if you do not think you can save very much, putting at least some money into such a plan will have a financial benefit.

Another way of paying for college ahead of time is through a Section 529 Prepaid Tuition Plan. The major benefit of this plan is that it allows you or your parents to lock in in-state tuition at public schools at current prices. If you purchase half a year's tuition, it will always be worth half a year's tuition, even five, 10, or 15 years later. Of course, this plan will only be worthwhile if you actually do attend a public school in your state. But if that is what you want, it can be a great way to avoid steep tuition increases, and attending a public school in your state is so much less expensive than being an out-of-state resident at a college in another state, as tuition rates can actually be tripled.

Like the 529 savings plan, prepaid tuition is now counted as a parental asset, so you can still qualify for financial aid even if all of your tuition is already paid for.

If you have been saving for a few years now, you may have a Coverdell Educational Savings Account (ESA). These accounts, often erroneously called Education IRAs, were created under the Taxpayer Relief Act of 1997. Anyone — grandparents, friends, or cousins — can contribute up to a total of $2,000 per year to these accounts. These accounts are treated as an asset of the owner for financial aid purposes. In most cases, this will be the parent, but ownership will pass to you when you reach age 18, unless provisions were made for your parents to retain ownership. The account will become your asset and could reduce your aid eligibility.

A disadvantage of the Coverdell accounts is that contributions are taxable, although withdrawals for higher education purposes are not.

Get a Job?

Should you get a job while you are still in high school and start putting away money for college? Although this sounds like the American way, and we all admire the student who works his or her way through college, the answer is no, if possible. Any income you earn over $3,000 is going to count against you and actually decrease the amount of financial aid you will be eligible to receive.

You are much better off spending your time studying, being involved in extracurricular activities, community service, and preparing your plan for college. These things will pay off big in the end by maximizing your financial aid and scholarship opportunities.

Looking Good on Paper

Part of preparing for college is to think about how your record is going to look to admissions and scholarship committees. Admissions officers and scholarship committees do not know you. The only things they know about you are what courses you have taken, the grades that you have earned, and the extracurricular and community service activities you have done (as long as you remember to include these things on the application). Since this is all they have to go on, you need to make yourself look great on paper. You might have the greatest leadership skills in the world, but unless you have actually held leadership positions in clubs or in school government, no one is going to know about it. Similarly, you might be a talented musician, chess player, debater, or you might have a driving passion for community service, but unless you can translate these skills and interests into some tangible accomplishments, your talents will go unnoticed, and your chances for scholarships will be scant. Competition for scholarships is going to be fierce, but if you have everything in place, you can bring home the money.

What to keep in mind to look your best on paper:

- Get copies of documents, awards, certificates, and other paperwork that proves that you completed, or were awarded, what you claim you did. Keep all of your paperwork together in a safe place, as you may need to refer to it again in your search for college funds, and even when applying for work in your field.

- Get names and contact information for those that can prove that you did what you claim. For instance, if you do volunteer work at a local community center, keep track of where it was (name, address, and phone number), and who your supervisor was. Your supervisor may be able to help later on with a letter of recommendation, or he or she may be a great personal contact for future needs, such as job hunting. Many schools now put your service hours on your transcripts, so be sure to document everything.

- Keep your contacts up to date even if you are no longer involved in a club or organization. It is in your best interest to keep the lines of communication open with those that you may need to contact later. You never know when you may need their assistance, whether they are providing you with work references writing letters of recommendation for scholarships or putting you in touch with someone that could help you in the future.

- Remember to include all of the above under the 'Activities' part of the college application. If you do not tell them what you were involved in, leadership positions or awards you may have, or even the number of community service hours, they will never know, as many schools do not have all of this information on the transcripts that will be sent to the colleges. This information needs to be put on all applications: college admissions and scholarships.

Grades

Keeping up your grade point average (GPA) is an absolute must. It is how you will be compared to others, and it can make or break your scholarship and college acceptance chances. Even a small increase in your GPA can make a difference of thousands of dollars. There are scholarships that do not consider grades, but the majority do require at least a B average, and we will cover those in a later chapter, but the safe path is to get good grades.

Good grades are one of the best investments in your future you can make. Some schools automatically hand out full scholarships to students with a certain GPA and SAT/ACT score. Even the schools that do not have full-ride academic scholarships often give a higher percentage of aid to students with high grades. Many schools give out merit scholarships, some regardless of need and some not.

Keeping your grades up for four years of high school requires a commitment on your part, but even if you did not do so well in your freshman and sophomore years, you can still bring your average up if you work at it. Any increase will be worth the effort.

Do not take the easy way out by avoiding challenging courses. It might be easier to make high grades in easy courses, but scholarship committees will take one look at your transcripts and not be impressed. When choosing your high school courses, follow your high school's college preparatory guidelines. Also, look at what the colleges you are interested in require of incoming freshmen as more colleges are considering the difficulty of your courses when making their decisions. Make sure you have covered all of the bases.

If you excel in a particular subject, such as math or history, make the most of it. Take the hardest courses your school offers in that subject and put forth your best effort.

SATs and ACTs

The SAT and the ACT are the most important tests you will take in high school. Every year there are calls for schools to rely less on standardized testing, but the reality is that the SAT and ACT are objective measurements schools can use to compare students from different backgrounds. Be sure to check your college's requirements on which test you need. Usually, it is only one or the other (your choice), but some colleges and scholarships may specify which one.

Many scholarship committees also rely heavily on SAT and ACT scores because they are a convenient way of comparing students from different backgrounds. Most merit scholarships are based simply on the highest scores and grade point average. Others will also look at the all-around picture, including your extracurricular and community service activities as well. Regardless, the higher your score, the higher your chance of winning thousands of dollars.

An excellent way to improve your chances of getting into the college you want, and getting it paid for, is to make the best possible score on the SAT or the ACT. If you are willing to invest four years of blood, sweat, and tears to keep up a killer GPA, why not invest six weeks to improve your SAT or ACT score? For students whose GPA is somewhat lacking, a high score is the single best way to overcome it.

Studies have shown that a test preparation course can increase a student's performance significantly. This can mean thousands of dollars in aid. It can also mean the difference between winning a big scholarship and being the runner-up. It could mean the difference between getting into a highly selective college and being left out in the cold.

Do some research before choosing a preparatory course. Some are expensive, while some are reasonably cheap or even free. A prep course is an investment, so do not choose a particular course simply because it has a lower cost. Some achieve big results, and others can give you a more modest increase. What you want to look for is a big increase, because it could not only mean thousands of dollars in scholarship money, but also a better chance of getting accepted into the college of your choice.

If you cannot find a course that is offered in your area, there are books available for purchase or in your local library that offer advice and practice tests. It is a good idea to consult these as the SAT or ACT approaches, even if you do take a prep course. These tests are that important.

There are also online sites that can help you prepare for these tests. For instance, College Board offers the SAT Preparation Center™ online at **www.collegeboard.com**, where you will find practice questions, practice tests, and other helpful information.

If you are still struggling with the SAT (or ACT) exam and worried about how to pass it with the highest score, or perhaps you are not a good test taker, you may want to consider a tutor who can offer you one-on-one assistance with your preparations.

Tests are important to pass with as high a score as possible, especially those that are designed for college entrance, such as the SAT and the ACT, and before every test you take you might want to consider the following:

- Prepare for the test. Study the materials beforehand. Do not wait until the last minute to do so.
- Try to relax and get a good night's sleep the night before your test.
- Read the test directions carefully.
- Read the questions carefully. If it is a multiple-choice test, look over every possible answer before deciding.
- Answer the questions you know first, then go over the ones that will take more time.
- Review your responses.
- Double check that you have answered all of the questions.
- Pace yourself.
- Answer every question on the ACT and, as of March 2016, the SAT as well. You still have a 20 percent chance of getting it right. So when they announce the final 10-minute call for each section, quickly answer every one of them.

It is a good idea to start taking the SAT and ACT the second half of your junior year. If the college(s) you are applying to accept either score, then you can, if needed, retake the one you did best on. You really want the best scores for college applications by late fall of your senior year. Many colleges have already accepted students by then, and if they give out freshmen scholarships (usually based on GPA and test scores) they are usually all given out by then as well.

CASE STUDY: ALEX FISHER, Owner of Crown Tutoring

The higher SAT score you have, the greater chance you will have of receiving scholarship awards from private sources and schools. Plus, the better chance you will have at being accepted into the best schools in the first place. Your SAT scores are the equivalent to all of your years of hard work in high school — they are that important. Not only are SAT scores considered a preview of how a test taker will do in college, they have become a yardstick for measuring life potential. Not necessarily fair, but it is true.

You should start studying as early as possible for the SAT by using review books, but if you feel you need extra help, you should enlist the help of an experienced tutor. It is worth every penny, as the payback for getting more financial aid, and a higher quality education, could be tenfold.

For instance, at Crown Tutoring you can receive in-home, one-on-one tutoring so you can learn in the comforts of your home. Experienced tutors are hired to help assist you with the SAT test, from learning about testing formats to following test directions to working on time management skills and taking short cuts that will help make standardized tests a breeze — whether you are studying for the SAT, the MCAT, the LSAT, GRE, or GED. Crown Tutoring will also recommend the necessary practice materials and implement a study regimen, as well as administer practice exams and evaluate the results to make sure you are on your way to passing your SAT with the highest score possible.

An ideal college applicant will be well-rounded with extracurricular activities, acts of citizenship, and leadership experiences, along with a solid GPA and high SAT score. Admissions offices look at the whole picture, but the SAT score is part of their evaluation. Of course, the amount that is awarded depends in part on how well the student filled out an application, how well they wrote an essay, and how much time they invested in searching for financial aid in the first place. So while you certainly need a good SAT score, you need to do the rest of the legwork as well.

By working with you to maximize your SAT score, you will have the extra edge you may need to get into the school that is first on your list and increase your possibilities to receive more grants and scholarships. Ultimately, that will lower how much you will have to pay back. The more prepared you are for the SAT test and the more comfortable you feel with test-taking, the better you will do on this very important test.

Activities

Extracurricular activities can be difficult to choose. Some academically gifted students would rather concentrate on their studies and feel that they do not have enough time to devote to anything else. But when it comes time to complete admissions and scholarship applications and you are staring at all those blank lines, you are going to wish you had participated in extracurriculars. Certainly, schools want motivated students who get the highest grades. But they are also looking for students with leadership or creative abilities and students who are willing to devote some time to making the world a better place. They want to have a well-rounded student body, with students of many abilities and talents.

There are all kinds of opportunities, both within your school and in the community, to get involved in. One of the best ways of getting attention is inventing your own project. This shows initiative and leadership — two qualities that colleges are always looking for.

Should you devote all of your time to one activity or get involved in as many activities as possible? The answer is somewhere in between. You might be interested in only one area, such as sports, writing, or photography. You might be the kind of student who likes to try different things but not stick with one particular activity very long. You might be a combination of the two.

Scholarship committees and admissions officers are going to look at both the range of your activities and the depth of your involvement, so it is better to have a mix to cover all of the bases. Find one activity that you enjoy, and go for mastery. If you like chess, join the chess club, take part in tournaments, and become an officer. Do other things, too, but show commitment. Mix it up a bit by becoming a member or officer of a club, playing on a sports team, or doing something that helps your community. The more variety the better. Not everyone, though, is meant to be an officer or play a sport. If that is the case, then just make sure that whatever you decide to do, do it with dedication. Taking on a new task is a challenge that will only help you grow, so don't give up before you at least try to do something new.

Do not forget to look outside the school as well. Many students make the mistake of thinking that only school-sponsored activities will count, but this is not true. Almost anything you do, including helping at your church, doing ham radio, or founding/participating in a local square-dance club will count, and it will help show who you truly are. If you are interested in health care, volunteer at a local hospital or nursing home. You will pick up some useful skills, as well as beef up your applications. Even better, organize a volunteer effort to help at the local nursing home. You will get points for leadership as well as for community service.

If your activities are heavily weighted toward one area, do some quick and simple activities to broaden your résumé. Your time is limited, and no one can do it all, so look for things you do in the community or school that will show your well-rounded skills.

Home-Schoolers

What can you do if you do not attend a regular school? The popularity of home school has exploded in recent years, and now more than one million students, or slightly more than 2 percent of all students, are home-schooled. In 2000, about half of the nation's colleges had a formal policy on admitting home-schoolers. Four years later, more than 80 percent of schools had one. Admissions officials and scholarship committees have become accustomed to making decisions about students with alternative records. Home-schooled students also enjoy a reputation as being well prepared for college, and they tend to score better on the SATs and other standardized tests than regular students. Admissions officials are well aware of this, but admissions policies vary by state, or even from school to school.

At some schools, you need to have all of the usual elements of a successful application. Harvard University, which accepts only a minimal number of home-schooled applicants, requires letters of recommendation, SAT/ACT scores, SAT II Subject Test scores from three subjects, a personal essay, and grades from any courses you have taken, which is the same that they would require of any student. The Massachusetts Institute of Technology has a similar policy.

Many schools are opening up the admissions process to better measure the alternative education that home-schoolers have received. The University of California at Riverside, for example, has recently adopted a policy that allows home-schooled students to submit a portfolio that details their coursework.

Talk to the admissions offices of schools you plan to attend by your junior year. Ask them what documentation they are going to require and what you can do to ensure that you will be accepted. Your school may have a policy in place, or they may be willing to work with you on an alternative application. The responsibility is going to be on you.

The big problem you are going to run into is that your mom or dad, or whoever has taught you, has given you grades for courses that only you took. In other words, there is no basis for comparison with other students, which admissions officers need in order to judge your worthiness. To put together a convincing application, you need to think about concrete ways that you can demonstrate your abilities so that they can be compared with others. Keep copies of tests you have taken, essays you have written, and research projects you have completed. This can show that you have learned the same material as public school students.

Of course, the most important thing you can do is to score well on the SAT/ACT. This is the most solid measurement that admissions and scholarship officials will have to compare you with others. If you can manage a near-perfect score, school officials are not going to care if were schooled at home, in Kathmandu, or under a rock. You are going to get accepted and get financial aid and scholarships based on the scores alone.

You also need to make friends with your local school system, because they can provide you with help. The guidance counselor can help when preparing for the SATs or ACTs, and completing other tasks. You should also be able to take part in extracurricular activities like sports, clubs, band, the school newspaper, or academic teams, if you so desire. Regulations on participation are handled locally, so you might have to do some negotiating. Start with the principal of your nearest high school. If you get no action, go next to the central office of the school system. If they will not budge, do not be afraid to take your case to the school board. Board members are usually elected community members, and they may be more sympathetic to your needs than school administrators. Plus, they have the power to change the rules.

If you do find that you are denied access to school activities, then you will need to fill the gap yourself. You do have the same opportunity as regular students to exhibit your leadership skills by spearheading community service projects or by finding other ways of demonstrating your leadership ability. You can also join recreational sports teams not related to the schools, as well as clubs or organizations. Your church is also a good place to start. Be sure that you can document these activities and the extent of your participation and leadership.

Also, you might be involved in an in-depth science or history project as part of your home schooling. These kinds of academic endeavors can help demonstrate your academic worth in lieu of grades. Keep copies of your schoolwork and projects in the event that you need to state your case in person before an admissions official.

Advanced Placement, IB, AICE, and CLEP

A great way to gain college credit while still in high school is through Advanced Placement (AP) courses or College-Level Examination Program (CLEP) exams. You can combine the two to get maximum punch.

Advanced Placement classes allow you to earn college credit for high school courses that you would take anyway. For example, instead of taking senior English and getting a course credit, take AP English and get the usual course credit plus the opportunity to earn college credit. The AP designation simply means that at the end of the course you can take a standardized exam for college credit. The College Board administers the AP program and testing. The higher your score, the more credit you earn. At this time, AP Exams are offered in 35 different subjects, including various sciences, calculus, statistics, computer science, English, seven different foreign languages, government and other social sciences, music theory, and studio art. Ask your school counselor about which courses are offered at your school and at what times. The cost of an AP Exam in 2016 is about $92, which is a real bargain compared to the cost of tuition.

If your school does not offer the course that you are interested in, there are two or three ways around this problem. One is to take the course at another school. This may involve some serious time management, but it is doable. Another option is to study for the exam on your own. There are test preparation books available for the AP Exams, just as there are for the SAT. There also might be an online course that you can take. Please note that the College Board will provide a $30 fee reduction for low-income students.

Be aware that these courses are designed to be taught at a college level, so they are going to move at a faster pace and cover more material than a regular high school class. In other words, do not try to do everything at once during your senior year. Take a couple of AP courses during your junior year and a couple more during your senior year. If you make high scores on the exams, you could be granted a half of a year's worth of college credit, which will cut your college costs by 12 to 25 percent. And you have gained high school credit to boot. Schools usually give you weighted points on the GPA scale for AP classes, so this will boost your overall ranking as well.

If you are not ready to take full advantage of this program, you can at least play to your strengths. If you excel in biology, then you are going to do well in AP biology. Do not pass on AP classes because you think they are only for the best students in your school. What it takes to succeed is effort, not genius. You are going to take these courses in a year or two anyway, so why not take advantage of an opportunity to get a head start? If these classes are too difficult, then perhaps you could try honors courses. You cannot use them for college credit, but they will still help prepare you for college curriculum.

Be aware, however, that not all schools accept AP credit, even though a huge majority does. The ones that do accept AP scores will generally accept up to one year's worth of credit. Check with the schools you plan to attend just to make sure.

Many schools also have the International Baccalaureate or AICE Program. You have to qualify to be accepted into these programs if a school in your county has them. If you take the classes and score well on their exams, you can earn up to 30 college credits from these programs. But you will still need to find out if the college of your choice will accept any or all of these credits.

The College Board also runs the CLEP program, but it is much broader in scope than the AP. CLEP tests are for anyone, regardless of ages or educational background. Each exam offers between 3-12 college credits, which are accepted by more than 2,000 colleges across the country. Again, check with the schools you plan to apply to about whether or not they will accept these credits. Many schools accept CLEP credits only in certain subjects. Each exam costs $80, which, like the AP Exam, is a real bargain. Exams are offered in a much broader range of areas than the AP, including such subjects as accounting, marketing, and human growth and development.

All of these programs are excellent ways to not only slash your college costs significantly but also help prepare you for college courses, and they are well worth the effort.

Community College Courses

Community colleges, and even four-year schools, are reaching out more than ever to nontraditional students. Courses are offered at branch campuses or online, and they are designed for evenings or summer. These are real college courses, so be prepared to devote the time and effort necessary to do a good job and keep up your grades. These will be the cheapest courses you are going to find, but keep in mind that since you are not a full-time student, you are not going to receive much financial aid. Many schools offer dual enrollment, which in most places is free. You take the classes during school hours (or evenings if you prefer), earning both high school and college credits at the same time. Some high schools even offer the college classes on their own campus. Students can go to both high school and college at the same time. Others can only attend dual enrollment classes during their last year of high school, assuming they have met all of the requirements. Remember that time spent working on night or online courses is time spent away from your high school courses or scholarship searches and that college classes will require more work than most high school classes. In other words, do not squander an opportunity to win a big scholarship so that you can knock out a few courses on the cheap.

These courses might work better for you in the summer, when you do not have the burdens of your regular schoolwork. Most schools have liberal admissions policies, so you might be able to take a couple of courses between your junior and senior years, and then a couple more between graduation and your first semester at college.

Another way that community colleges can save you money is the transfer trick. You can complete your first two years at an inexpensive community or junior college and then transfer to the college of your choice to complete your degree. You can save many thousands of dollars this way, especially if you live at home while attending, and you will still end up with exactly the same degree. Many times, living is costlier than the college tuition and fees itself.

Community college is also a good stepping stone as far as difficulty level is concerned. Envision steps, with the bottom one (and easiest to navigate) being high school. The next level would then be community college, where the difficulty range is harder. Then you have the top step — a four-year university — the hardest to climb. In other words, community college is a step up from high school but helps prepare you even more for those 300-500 students per class colleges. If your grades or test scores prevent you from being accepted into the university of your choice, you will have a fresh start with a community college. Work to keep those grades high, and it will make the transfer process doable.

If you are considering going to a community college, keep in mind the following:

- Make sure that you check articulation agreements that your community college might have with the four-year college or university that you are interested in. You want to make sure that your credits will transfer to your four-year degree and that you are taking the correct classes needed for your major.

- If you have a major in mind, you might want to look at several community colleges and see which one best prepares you for your ongoing education. For instance, if you are going to major in math, you would want to pick a community college that best prepares you with plenty of math classes.

- If you do not know what your future plans are in terms of degree choice, it might be best to choose an Associate in General Studies degree program, where you would study many different subjects and work to figure out what most appeals to you.

- Even during your first few years of college, whether you are sure of your major or not, you should meet with an academic adviser at your school to help you determine your right course of action and how to get there.

Wrapping It Up

Few students can do it all, but every student can at least do something to get prepared for college. The important thing is to set a goal and prepare a plan for reaching it. You can do many things while you are still in high school that will pay off big when it is time to pack for college. For instance, you can work on taking higher-level courses and increasing your grades. You can start your scholarship and grant search early. You can develop a savings plan. You can research potential schools. You can look into community colleges in your area. You can have a heart-to-heart talk with your parents to see how much they would be willing to help out — even if it means letting you live at home. Planning for college takes time and effort, but you will be glad you devoted yourself to it.

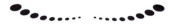

Chapter 2

Applications

As you begin your senior year in high school, it is time to start gathering information on colleges you are interested in and begin making choices. There are many reasons to choose a school, including finding one that offers your field of studies, finding one that offers the most reasonable tuition, or choosing one that is based on location. This chapter will help guide you through the process of choosing the right school so that you will be off to a good start in life.

Choosing the Right College

You are about to make an investment in yourself. A good place to research higher education is a comprehensive guide to colleges, such as The Princeton Review's *Complete Guide to Colleges* and the College Board's *Book of Majors* and *College Handbook*. Also consult some of the rankings guides, such as the annual special issues of *U.S. News and World Report* magazine.

Criteria for choosing a school are: Does the school meet your educational needs? For example, if you are interested in the sciences, you should look at colleges that have strong science programs. If you are interested in marine biology, is there a lab to offer you real-world experience? If you want to study foreign languages, do they offer a semester abroad or a similar program? How qualified are the teachers? How many different foreign language courses are offered?

How comfortable will you be in a particular school environment? For instance, schools sponsored by religious organizations may impose behavioral restrictions, extensive coursework in Bible studies, or mandatory church attendance during the week. A larger school offers anonymity and independence, while smaller schools are like small towns — everyone knows everyone. Large universities have a variety of majors, while smaller schools may offer your specialty. Remember too, that many students tend to change their major for many different reasons, but a college with a larger assortment will open more options if you do change your mind.

Consider the school's reputation. Graduating from a top-ranked school can open career doors. Corporate recruiters and graduate school committees do take a degree from a prestigious school seriously. Of course, your own performance is going to carry a great deal of weight, no matter what school you attend, but apply to the best schools you can.

Will you be employable when you graduate? Check out the job placement record for your chosen major. Do graduates land jobs with the top companies in your field? How many graduates go on to get their master's, doctorate, or law degree? What is the internship program for your major? Many times career opportunities rely on that more than anything, as the internship can be the proverbial foot in the door in getting hired with that company.

And of course, can you afford to go there? If other less expensive colleges offer your major, then you might be better off attending them. Although you may need to turn to loans, the fewer the better. Too many adults end up paying off student loans for too long a time, and by the time they are paid off, they have actually doubled the amount they took out. If you do not receive financial aid in grants or scholarships, then living at home or attending community or in-state colleges are ways to help avoid this.

Are you willing to attend? Worst-case scenario: attend for two years and transfer.

Visit Campuses

Before you settle on one school, visit the campus for a couple of days. Since you are going to spend two to four years (or possibly more) and make a considerable financial investment, it is a good idea to make sure it is right for you. Your first impression from a lovely website may dissolve when you meet the students, or your bad impression from the school's literature may change when you are on-site. Visiting the actual college can completely change your mind, as each college has a personality of its own.

Before you arrive, prepare a list of questions that can help you decide if the school is right for you. Your list might include:

- How much can you expect to pay for rent and utilities for off-campus housing?
- What types of scholarships or grants are offered?

- Are part-time jobs available near campus?
- What is the availability and cost of public transportation, both off- and on-campus?
- Do other students look like those you want to spend your next few years with? Does it seem to be a close-knit community? What is the cultural diversity of the student body?
- Can you imagine yourself on campus? Does it feel right?
- Is there campus security available, especially for night classes? You might ask about the crime rate.
- What is on the bulletin boards and in the college papers? What kinds of topics are the students discussing?
- What does the campus look like? Is it clean or dirty? New or rundown?
- How large are the classes?
- What services does the school offer? Job placement? Academic advising? Internships?
- What is the quality of the teachers? What is their education level? Do assistants teach classes? What is the average number of students per class?
- What are some of the extracurricular activities?

Cost

Should you receive financial aid to attend college, it is possible (though not likely) that a private school will turn out to cost the same as a state school. Apply to all schools that you like, and apply to every possible source of financial help. As a precaution, choose a fallback school, one where you are guaranteed admittance, and one that you can afford. It should also be affordable so that you can attend and get your degree should you get only a small amount of loans.

Calculating the real cost

Once you have narrowed your choices down and have some idea of where you are headed, it is time to face the reality of finances. How much is this going to cost you? This is where some careful thought and planning can save you some pain later on. Most people tend to underestimate the cost of college because they fail to include all of the expenses they are going to encounter. Check out the catalogs or websites of colleges you plan to apply to in order to get the basic costs. Many college websites now have the 'college cost calculator' to help you with this.

- **Tuition:** A big up-front cost is, of course, tuition (and built-in fees). This is the money the college charges you to attend classes, and it is usually based on a semester or quarter hour. A few colleges may have a discount for full-time students. Remember that tuition tends to increase about 8 percent per year, so if you are planning a couple of years in advance, adjust this cost accordingly.

- **Fees:** This can be a tricky one. Colleges charge a variety of fees for all kinds of services. First, there are the fees that are built into the tuition-per credit hour. These fees include things such as transportation access, technology, sports, and activities. Other costs may be incurred if you plan to take many science courses, where you should expect to pay lab fees. Parking fees vary widely. At rural colleges, where lots of parking is available, permits are cheap. However, at urban schools, where space is a premium, you might have to pay as much as $500 per year for the privilege of driving your car. You will also have to pay a health fee, which covers doctor's visits at the school's clinic. Be sure to read over carefully what the health fee does and does not cover. For example, you usually have to pay full price for prescriptions unless you have insurance.

- **Books:** College textbooks are notoriously expensive. Costs vary by course, but you can expect to pay $300-$500 per semester. You are also going to need notebooks, pencils and pens, a calculator (and sometimes the graphing one which runs $100 or more), and the usual school supplies.

- **Living expenses (on-campus):** If you choose to live in a dormitory, living expenses are easy to figure. Just be sure to check if the meal plan includes weekends (often they do not), and calculate accordingly. Find out if the meal plan rolls over if you do not use it. Is it for three meals a day, seven days a week, or is it just nine or 15 meals per week? Also, if you plan to stay in the dorms during the summer, there will be an additional charge.

- **Living expenses (off-campus):** These expenses can vary according to location. Guidelines might be available from the school you plan to attend, or from organizations such as the Chamber of Commerce of the city where the college is located. In any case, you should include the cost of rent, utilities, phone and internet service, and groceries. You should also include any deposits you will have to pay, including those for utilities, which can be considerable for first-time renters. If you have a roommate, these expenses can be cut in half or more. There are often many quads or apartments that are near schools and rented out to college students by private businesses or people. These usually include electricity, water, cable, etc. Not only are they much less expensive then dorms, but you get some privacy as you usually have a room to yourself and only have to share a bathroom with one other person.

- **Computer:** These days, a computer is a necessity. For the greatest flexibility, you should choose a laptop. You can take it with you to classes, to the library, home with you on the weekends or on breaks, or wherever you need. Most schools offer free computer labs that you can use, but the inconvenience generally is not worth it. When choosing a computer, you should get one with enough memory and speed to get you through four years of college. Do not skimp on performance just to save a few dollars because it may cost you in the long run. Look for a processor with a speed of at least 2 GHz and a hard drive with at least 120 GB of memory. You should also consider the cost of software as well, which is going to vary according to which major you choose to study.

- **Clothes and entertainment:** This is where a lot of your disposable income is going to go, but it can be difficult to budget. Ask your parents what they spend on your clothing per year to get some idea of how much you can expect to spend. You are also going to want to have some fun, and fun usually costs money. College towns have many opportunities for you to eat, drink, and be merry but also many opportunities to leave you broke. Be sure to include some money for the occasional splurge.

- **Insurance:** Generally, your parents' health insurance will continue to cover you while you are in school, and if they have a family plan there is no additional cost to keep you signed up. If you are not covered, you should consider getting your own health insurance. Costs vary, and many colleges offer an affordable plan designed specifically for students.

- **Phone and cable TV:** You are probably going to be paying for the convenience of a smart phone. It is actually a luxury, not a necessity, but everyone has become so used to carrying one around that they think they are a necessity. The same goes for cable TV, though with the advent of other movie-streaming services such as Netflix™ and Hulu™, you can get away with paying less. Chances are, your dorm room is going to have a common area with a TV, but for most people, having their own remote is as necessary as underwear.

- **Household items:** Whether you are living in the dorms or an apartment off campus, you are going to have to consider the essentials of daily life. You can probably bring some of this from home, provided your parents will let you, but be sure to estimate the cost of what you may have to purchase.

  - ↠ Blankets, sheets, towels, and washcloths
  - ↠ Basics: soap, deodorant, shampoo, toothpaste, and other grooming products
  - ↠ Appliances, such as a coffee maker, small microwave oven, and toaster (or toaster oven)
  - ↠ Food if you do not live in the dorms, or your meal plan does not cover all of your meals

Add all of these figures, and try to think of anything else you might need, or anything else you will be doing that will require extra money.

These expenses can add up to a scary total that goes way beyond tuition, which is scary enough. It is better, though, to overestimate what college is going to cost and be prepared for it than to underestimate and find yourself short of funds. If you know what you are going to have to spend, you can better set your financial aid goals.

It is important to do this exercise for each school to which you are going to apply. Costs vary widely, and you cannot assume that the price of a dorm room at one school is going to be same as the price at another. Many schools even charge different prices based on which dorm you end up living in. The more expensive ones usually have more amenities, such as a larger or private bedroom, less people to the bathrooms, and even a gym. But again, do you need all of this? Is it worth the extra costs?

Keep in mind, though, that there are many ways to cut these costs or at least keep them under control. The following chapters are full of tips for finding money and cutting expenses.

A good way to feel better about the cost of going to college is to consider the cost of not going to college. One of the practical benefits of education is that it increases your earning power. Considering that you are going to be out in the world earning money for about four decades, even a modest difference in annual income can make a huge difference in your life. According to the National Center for Education Statistics in 2015, college graduates earn 62 percent more than those without a degree. Over a lifetime, a college degree can mean more than a million dollars in extra income. In other words, in spite of the high cost of a college education, it remains the best investment you can make in yourself.

There are also many professions that require you to have a degree. Even if you end up doing something else with your life than what you studied in college, your degree is going to open doors for you your whole life that would otherwise remain closed.

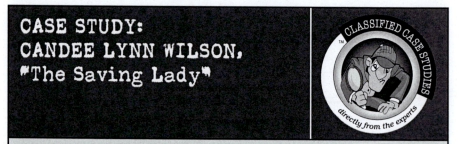

CASE STUDY: CANDEE LYNN WILSON, "The Saving Lady"

During my 64 years, I have been a starving student, single parent, sole breadwinner, and self-employed — a recipe for a saving train wreck. My father was a hard worker, but his attitude toward money went something like, "If you cannot do something first-class, do not do it at all." My mother, an extremely frugal-minded woman, was always bailing my father out of financial disasters.

Unfortunately, my mother never passed on to me her saving secrets. I was left to discover those by trial and error. I hope I can make a difference in someone's financial future by passing on what I have learned through my website and blog.

Following is some general saving advice that will not only get you through college but also the rest of your life.

- Consider a local community college for your first two years of study. You will pay much less for your prerequisite courses. If a community college is not an option, check in-state or public schools where tuition will be substantially less than a private college or university and entry requirements will usually be more liberal.

- School housing is a huge expense, so look at schools in your own community or in a different city or state where you have a friend or relative with whom you can make a living arrangement. You might not think it is cool to live with your parents or old-maid aunt during college, but you will come to appreciate the money it saves. Zip up your pride and you could avoid really big student loans. Plan on working part time to reduce costs. This means not loading up on credit hours that leave you no time for anything except study and play. A school/work/play schedule will teach you time management and prepare you for a point in the future when part-time work may just bail you out of a temporary financial jam.

- Learn to take public transportation, ride a bike, or walk. The cost of maintaining a car is a big drain on the pocketbook. If you must have a car, buy a good used one for little money, paying cash so you can minimize the cost of insurance by only carrying liability coverage. Even when you can afford to buy a car, always pay cash and never buy new.

- Look for used textbooks online at sites like **www.amazon.com**, **www.textbooks.com**, **www.bookbyte.com**, or **www.half.ebay. com/textbooks**. When you are finished with them, go back and resell them online to recoup part or all of your investment. Buying "recycled" furniture, clothing, household items, etc. is not only frugal, but also "green."

Public or Private?

One of the options you will have to consider when choosing a school is whether to attend a private school or a state-funded college. There are advantages and disadvantages to each.

A diploma from a private school traditionally carries more prestige than one from a public school, but this is mainly the Ivy League schools, such as Harvard, Princeton, MIT, and Brown. Recruiters and graduate school committees have customarily looked favorably upon such private schools. However, as with any degree, there are no guarantees. A fancy pedigree may not help you succeed. Keep in mind that many state schools have established reputations as good as, or better than, private colleges.

As always, before you decide on a school because of its name recognition, do your homework. Consult the college ratings guides, and make sure the reality matches the hype. You might find some surprises.

Private schools can offer options or alternative curricula that are not available at public schools. Small private schools are often founded with guiding principles or beliefs that set them apart. Smaller schools have also made themselves more attractive (and therefore competitive) by offering small class sizes, unusual course requirements, or interesting social programs. If you are the kind of person who likes to wander off the beaten track, then a private school might get you there.

The reason many students do not consider applying to private schools is that they are more expensive than public schools. Private schools' costs may be more reasonable than you think. While their tuition costs may be higher, often private schools have more scholarships and grants to offer their students, and once you factor those into the bottom line, you may realize that a private school education may be more affordable. At the same time, many of these private schools will offer huge scholarships that only make a small dent in the costs. When the total cost comes into play, oftentimes their tuition is so high that you will still end up paying much more to go there than a public school.

Many of the Ivy League schools are more easily affordable if you are in financial need. Princeton was one of the first to do this, and more now follow this path. Of course, you still have to meet the requirements to be accepted, but quite a few private schools do not want their students to have loans and will give them scholarships and grants to help cover the costs. They will still look at what the FAFSA considers to be the parents' contribution, so this all relies on having a low income.

There is also a way to obtain a prestigious private school degree without the expense of paying four years of private school tuition. You can earn two years of credit at an inexpensive public school and then transfer to a more expensive dream school to finish your degree. You end up with the same diploma you would have received had you attended all four years. Be careful, though, to check out the school's policy on transfers. Most schools limit the number of transfer students they will accept and require a respectable grade point average. There is no guarantee that you are going to get in, but this is an option for those who want the cachet a private school diploma can bring without the cost. To help your chances of acceptance, contact the person in charge of your major's department. Let them know what your plans are, and ask them what classes they would advise you to take. Contact them at the beginning of each year to let them know you are still interested and for any other advice they may have for being accepted into their program.

In-State or Out-of-State?

What if you choose the public school route but the school you want to attend is in a different state? Many state schools have established excellent academic reputations that rival the best private schools, so if prestige is at the top of your list of criteria for choosing a school, this might be a worthwhile option for you. An out-of-state public school might also offer a certain program of study that is not available in your state.

Be prepared to pay. Public schools are funded in part by tax dollars, so if you live in a different state you will be expected to pay this portion as additional tuition. Residency requirements vary by state, and most states have toughened up their policies in recent years. Out-of-state tuition can actually be three times the amount of in-state tuition.

Some top-notch out-of-state schools (also known as public ivies) are better bargains than others are. Tuition at the University of Michigan and the University of Vermont, for example, has become as expensive as private school for out-of-state students, at $40,000 for Vermont and $43,476 a year for Michigan, but other schools are relatively cheap by comparison.

If it truly is your dream to attend an out-of-state school, ask the school's financial aid office about residency requirements as early as you can, in case it might be possible for you to meet them. Some schools allow you to establish residency after you have attended for a certain period, but generally this involves living off-campus. You will probably also be required to file a tax return in that state and register your car there. Before all this happens, be prepared to work extra hard to come up with additional funds. Some schools have out-of-state tuition waivers, which you should ask about. If the school is still too expensive but has the best program for you, then think about attending a local community or four-year college, then transfer after you have your two-year degree.

Location Matters

The type of environment that the school is located in can have a great effect on the cost of your education. Rent tends to be high for schools located in urban areas. Schools that are located in smaller towns tend to have the lowest cost of living. If you plan to live off-campus and money is tight, this should be a real consideration in your choice of schools.

Location also has a big effect on your transportation costs. If you plan to drive home often, the farther away you are the more it is going to cost. If the school is too far away to drive, you will probably want to fly home several times a year, which can be costly.

If you do not have or want to have to buy a car, you may want to consider what kind of public transportation is available. Check with the city's transportation department to see if buses are readily available and how often they run. You might want to see how often they come and go near your school. A few cities, such as New York, San Francisco, and Chicago offer the added bonus of being able to take trains and cabs, if you can afford them. Other commuting issues will be presented later in this book.

An additional consideration for location is climate. If you are accustomed to the sunny warmth of Florida, a Wisconsin winter is going to be a real shock. If you prefer a mild climate, then you are not going to enjoy the heat and humidity of South Carolina. It seems like a small consideration, but remember, you are going to have to live there for four years. Plus, if you do not have the clothing, that is another consideration. If you live in a warm climate and do not have warm sweaters, jackets, boots, and mittens, that can add up to hundreds of dollars that you have to dole out just to go to college.

Living at Home

One of the best ways to cut the cost of attending college is to live at home. This option is not for everyone, of course. Some students do not live within commuting distance of a desirable college. Most students, though, simply do not want to live at home. Being on your own is part of the college experience and is one that many students loathe giving up. There definitely are advantages to living on-campus or near school: friendships are easier to make and sustain, and you will feel more a part of the college community.

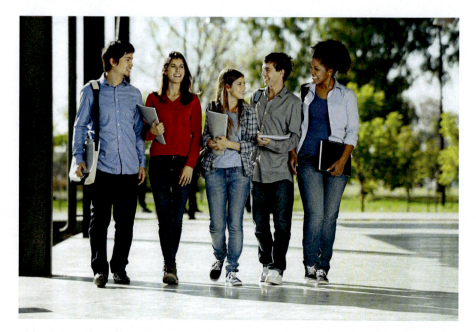

The main advantage to living at home is that your parents are probably footing the bills. You will pay no rent or dorm fees, utilities, or perhaps even food. Many times, living can cost much more than tuition. If you do decide to face the situation and go it on the cheap, there are some hazards to watch out for. Although it may be less costly living at home and going to school, it may not necessarily be easy.

If your parents are pressed for cash, you may want to consider making an arrangement with them that you pay rent for living at their house. The rent, no doubt, would still be less than if you were out on your own somewhere else, and you can enjoy the comforts of home while pursuing your education.

Another thing that students do not realize is if they live at home while attending college, they are seldom there. Whether it's attending classes, studying at the library, working on school projects, or working, the time at home becomes minimal.

Commuter Blues

Driving to school can be a real burden. Parking is the first problem. Most schools grow faster than their parking lots, which means when school begins in the fall you might find yourself driving onto curbs or parking your car in the street to make it to class because there are no spaces available. The situation tends to ease in the afternoon and evening, when fewer students are in class. This schedule could take some getting used to, but it will relieve many headaches for you. An additional option is to take the earliest classes, which are not very popular. This will get you into a parking space before the rush begins at 9 a.m.

Keep in mind that commuting to school is not free. First, with the price of gas fluctuating, the daily drive to campus can get expensive. Estimate the number of miles you are going to drive each week, including weekend trips to the library or home, and calculate how much fuel is going to cost. Also, keep in mind that commuting is going to add wear and tear to your vehicle. You are going to do this for four years, so you are going to need regular maintenance such as oil changes, along with some major expenses such as a new set of tires. You are also going to need a reliable car to begin with. If your car breaks down during finals week, you are going to have to do a lot of explaining to your professors, who will not be very sympathetic.

With these words of caution in mind, commuting might still be the best option for you. Not everyone lives down the street from their dream school, but most people live within driving distance of at least one college, and it still ends up being less expensive than living on your own.

Online Options

One way to avoid the commute to school is to take online classes. The number of internet options has exploded in recent years. They were originally designed for nontraditional students because students who had full-time jobs and a family needed greater flexibility than on-campus courses could offer. Nowadays, even traditional students are signing on because of that same flexibility. The classes operate in a number of ways. Some courses require at least some contact with the professor in a classroom setting, usually at the beginning of the term. Thereafter, students do most of the work on their own, checking in with the professor and their class through an online chat room. Work can be assigned and turned in through the internet. Testing varies. In some cases, exams have to be proctored by an approved person, while other courses require a trip to a real classroom where everyone takes the test together.

If you are interested in completing much of your coursework this way, be sure to check out all of the curriculum requirements thoroughly to make sure that you are not going to run into any problems. These should be listed on the course website, and you can always check with the professor to be sure. If you have research projects, you could end up spending so much time driving to the library or the lab that you might as well have taken on-campus classes. Your local public library cannot compete with a college library that caters to students by subscribing to specialized journals and ordering books and other research materials.

You also need to make sure that you have the motivation to get the work done on time without a great deal of prompting. Some students need teacher interaction to learn. Your ability to succeed in an online course may depend on the subject matter. If you usually have trouble with English or math, you may be better off in the classroom.

Also, you need to have a place to work free of distractions. Younger brothers and sisters, friends, and even parents can get in the way. A bedroom or an office that is quiet and isolated from all of the things going on in the rest of the house would be ideal.

An option that has become available in recent years is to earn an online degree offered by a for-profit college. A for-profit college is a corporation, like the University of Phoenix, that offers accredited degrees just as a nonprofit college does. These schools have catered to graduate students in the past, particularly for business degrees, but they are now moving into the undergraduate arena. Check it out the same as you would a traditional brick-and-mortar college. Pay special attention to financial aid to make sure they can offer you aid other than student loans. Find out about their graduation rates, and examine which companies actively recruit their graduates. Are they going to offer you the same job placement assistance that traditional schools do? Finally, make sure they are accredited in your major. Just because they are accredited to grant master's degrees in business does not mean that their social work program for undergraduates is also accredited, and a degree from a college with no accreditation is as almost as good as no degree.

You are likely to run into the same issues with online universities as you will with online courses offered by a traditional college. Your online school probably does not have a library, except what they have online. The internet offers an incredible array of online journals and books, but it is still no match for a well-funded college library. Plus, if you are gathering several sources to work with, you are going to have a much easier time if you can lay everything out on the desk and put it all together. Working with multiple websites and writing a paper at the same time is awkward, to say the least. Physical libraries have one other advantage: well-trained and experienced librarians who can help you.

You also need to find out how many trips you are going to have to make to the main campus or corporate office. Depending on the school's location, transportation expenses can add up quickly. Frequent-flyer miles are great but not if the cost of airfare puts you out of school entirely.

Any way you choose to do it, getting online can be a hassle-free way of getting the coursework done. For commuters, it can make the college experience easier and provide some welcome flexibility throughout your college years.

Choosing the right college is more complicated than it sounds, but some effort now will pay off big in the end. Once you know where you are headed and have a realistic idea of what it will take to get you there, you can get the ball rolling.

To make shopping around for your online education easier, several search engines are designed to help you find the best opportunity for you to pursue your degree.

- Monster's Learning Network includes a source to help you find the right school, whether it is undergraduate, graduate, or post-graduate. According to them, "We provide information on prominent, accredited online schools and online degrees." To start your search, visit: **http://onlineschools.net**.

- Guidetoonlineschools.com is "an education directory specializing in online degrees, online schools, and distance learning." To start your search, visit: **www.guidetoonlineschools.com**.

- Directory of Schools assists students who are seeking online degrees and education via distance learning and campus colleges. The site features 6,765 accredited online degrees and

13,578 campus-based degree programs. To start your search, visit: **http://directoryofschools.com**.

Of course, there are many more sites that can help you find the right online school, and you might want to conduct a search on a few of them.

The Application Process

Once you have decided on which schools to apply to, the next step is to fill out the applications. Usually this is a straightforward process, but it can be time consuming. Most applications require about the same information, so keep a folder for each school and make copies of everything, including admissions essays. This will prevent you from having to repeat your work for each school. Also, pay attention to admission deadlines. They can vary greatly from school to school.

The admission packets are usually composed of some or all of these elements:

- **The application:** For the majority of schools, the application can be completed online, but if you are using the paper version, be sure to use a typewriter. Handwritten applications look sloppy and can be difficult to read. Be sure to fill out the forms completely and answer all of the questions.

- **The transcripts:** These will need to be sent from your high school. It will be easier to send them all at once so that you do not overlook anything. You also want get a copy for yourself so that you can look them over carefully before sending them. Mistakes, such as incorrect grades or missing courses, have been known to occur.

- To order transcripts you can contact your schools directly. Some offer order forms online. Other times, you can write to them with a signed request. If you are requesting one from your high school, many times they can send the ones in the same state electronically at no cost to you. There is generally a small fee from colleges of around $5 per transcript. You can also order transcripts from The National Student Clearinghouse, described as "the nation's trusted source for post-secondary and secondary student degree, diploma, and enrollment verification." Contact them at **www.studentclearinghouse.org**.

- **Recommendations:** Choose people in authority who know you well and who you think will not only write a positive essay for you but also get it done on time. A great recommendation is not going to do you any good if the admissions office never gets it. Good choices are teachers, administrators, guidance counselors, and ministers. If you have held a job for a while and done well, talk to your boss about writing one of the letters. Admissions officials are impressed by a good work ethic. Many state-funded schools do not want or require letters of recommendations, so do not send them if not asked for. If it (or anything else) is listed as "optional," then by all means send it. This is one way to see how much it means to you to go to their college.

- **The essay:** Be honest. Do not pad your achievements. You want to highlight your accomplishments and the talents that you actually possess. What the admissions office is looking for is whether you are a good fit for their school, so keep in mind why you chose to apply to that school in the first place. If you have had an obstacle that you had to overcome in life, this is the time to tell about it. You are not doing this for pity. You are writing to let them know you have faced something difficult in life and did not let it get in your way. If you have done your homework and chosen schools that match your needs, the essay will not be a problem. Finally, have several people read it and offer suggestions for improvement. Your English teacher or guidance counselor would be a good choice. They can catch mistakes and polish your essay so that you look as good as possible. Remember: spell check does not catch everything.

- **The interview:** Most colleges do not require an interview because it is not practical, but there is a chance that you are going to find yourself in front of an admissions officer at some point. Some more prestigious colleges may even have alumni that live in your area interview you. Dress nicely, and be prepared to answer the questions honestly and in a straightforward manner. You should already know why you want to attend that particular school and why you would be an asset for them. Prepare a few personal stories that reveal episodes of your life that taught you an important lesson or were growth experiences for you. If the interviewer questions your grades or SAT score, admit your shortcomings, and discuss how you are working to overcome them. Also remember to look them in the eye when speaking to them. When answering a question, do not just say yes or no, but give a reason for your answer. Talking too little can be as harmful as talking too much.

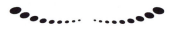

Wrapping It Up

Once the applications are submitted online or in the mail, an important step toward college has been completed. Hopefully, the process of choosing a school has helped you find out more about yourself and what you want to do in life. As you wait on the acceptance letters or emails, you still have much to do and are not going to have time to rest. The next stage is financial aid, which will help you pay for the college of your dreams.

In the meantime, you could be visiting campuses, looking at your budget to see where you might be able to cut costs, and looking at online options as a possibility instead of waiting for the acceptance decision to arrive.

Chapter 3

The Numbers Game

he Free Application for Federal Student Aid (FAFSA) is one of the most important applications you will encounter. Schools, government agencies, and many scholarship committees use the Student Aid Report (SAR) to determine need, which determines how much money you are going to get in aid. This chapter walks you through this process and offers tactics and tips to maximize your benefits. Understanding how financial aid officers and others determine your need is the best way to ensure that you get all that you deserve.

Private colleges may use a different financial aid application alongside the FAFSA, called the College Board's CSS/Financial Aid PROFILE application. Some colleges require additional forms that have to be filled out and sent directly to that school. In short, you have to find out for each school that you are applying to exactly what their requirements are for financial aid applications.

You are not going to know the exact amount of financial aid you are going to receive until April, but you can get a rough estimate now, which might help you in planning, through the link on the FAFSA website called the 4caster. There you can get an estimate of your potential grant money. Your financial need is the Cost of Attendance (COA), minus your Expected Family Contribution (EFC), which is the amount that you and your family are expected to pay out of pocket for your education. The goal here is to follow strategies to reduce your EFC to the minimum, which will increase the amount of aid you will be eligible to receive. Here is the good news: Your EFC does not increase if the COA increases, so if you choose a more expensive school, you may actually be eligible for more aid.

Worksheets are available online at **www.finaid.org/calculators**. These can help you get organized and learn how the process works.

What Is the FAFSA?

The FAFSA is a form that documents important facts about you and your family's financial situation, including income and assets. Essentially, colleges have an allotted amount of money for all of their students, and they use FAFSA to ration aid to the families who need it most.

Even if you think that you are not going to be eligible for aid, it is wise to apply anyway. There is no objective way to tell if you are going to be turned down, and the amount you receive can depend on many factors. For example, if your family has multiple children in college, your chances of winning aid increase considerably. Also, as tuition and the other costs of attending college continue to rise, the number of families eligible for aid increases. So, if you are not eligible for aid your freshman year, rising costs may make you eligible your sophomore, junior, or senior year. The only way you are going to know is to fill out the forms and complete the process. Also, many college scholarships require you to fill out the FAFSA to see whether or not you are receiving any grants, as those not eligible for financial aid usually still need the extra scholarship money.

Families in the upper income brackets — even more than $250,000 a year — can still benefit from the FAFSA. You are not going to get Pell Grants, but you will be eligible for unsubsidized student loans, such as the Stafford and PLUS loans, which might be a good option for you. You will not be eligible for these loans without a FAFSA, and they are usually one of the lower interest rate loans you can get for college students.

Private scholarships that are based all or in part on your financial needs may also use the FAFSA as the basis for their decisions. For this reason, keep careful records and copies of everything connected with your financial aid application.

You have to do this for every year you attend college, so the more you know about it, the better you will be able to maximize your financial aid opportunities.

Filing Tips

You can start on the FAFSA after Jan. 1 of your senior year (although this is going to change for the 2017-2018 FAFSA), and you do not have to wait until your family's taxes are done before you can complete the job. You can even start the FAFSA pre-application process in November to give you a head start. You can print out the pre-application and fill it in by hand to help you organize the information you will need on the FAFSA, but when it is actually time to submit it, it is preferable to a do it online.

The FAFSA form is available from many sources, but the best way to do it is online. Your results will be sent to you and the colleges much faster if you complete the online form, and the IRS Data Retrieval Tool, which FAFSA uses to work with your income, also makes the procedure much easier. Another reason to use the Retrieval Tool is that approximately 30 percent of all FAFSAs are selected for verification (where the student/parent must provide paper proof of everything), and the ones that do not use the IRS Data Retrieval Tool are usually the first ones chosen.

If you still prefer to do the hard copy, you can get the paper version from the financial aid office at any college, possibly the public library, or by calling 1-800-4-FED-AID (1-800-433-3243). You can also go online while you are in your sophomore or junior year and use the 4Caster link to get an idea of what your EFC will be.

When filing online, go to at **http://fafsa.ed.gov**. This method has several advantages over the paper version. Just like filing taxes online, filing your FAFSA online will get you your SAR a few weeks earlier than if you used the paper version. The web version also has a built-in error-check system and makes it easier to file a Renewal FAFSA, which you have to do every year.

In the past, the web version required that you get a Personal Identification Number (PIN). But in 2016, you will no longer use PIN numbers. Instead, you will create a Federal Student Aid ID with a username and password, as will your parents. Parents will be able to use the same username and password for all of their children.

One of the most important things to remember is what FAFSA (Free Application for Federal Student Aid) stands for so that you will go to the correct website. If you Google search FAFSA, the first link that comes up will be FAFSA.com (not .gov). This is a website that will try to charge you $90 or more for the free application.

When you are ready to start, you need to get your financial documents together. You are going to need, at a minimum:

- Your driver's license and social security card
- Your income tax returns for the previous year
  - ¤ If you are married, your spouse's returns
- Your parents' income tax returns for the previous year
- Your parents' social security numbers
- Recent bank statements
- Statements relating to stocks, bonds, mutual funds, money market accounts, prepaid tuition plans, Section 529 savings plans, Coverdell Education Savings Accounts, and other investments

- Statements showing nontaxable income such as Veteran's Benefits, Social Security income, or AFDC
- Family-owned business and farm records

Deadlines for filing the FAFSA vary by state and college, so be sure to check with the financial aid departments of the schools you are applying to. The FAFSA website at **https://fafsa.ed.gov** also maintains a list of state deadlines. Most deadlines are around March 1, but the goal should be to complete the form by Feb. 15. Each college has a certain amount of money that they will give out in grants, and if you are late, most of the money may already be gone, and you might not get your fair share.

If your family's taxes are not done by then you will have to estimate based on end-of-year pay stubs, the previous year's tax return, or some other method. This is likely to happen as many firms do not have W-2s ready until the end of January, and you may have to wait even longer on 1099s and other documents you need. If you pay someone to prepare and file your taxes, you might have a longer wait, especially if your taxes are complicated and your preparer is buried in work. File the FAFSA anyway. Even if you are self-employed, you should have a close idea of what you made for the year. You can always make corrections later once your taxes have been filed. An alternative is to file your taxes early and then make any corrections with an amended return, but this could add an unnecessary complication to your life. Just make sure you get the FAFSA done on time. If your parents refuse to do it until their taxes are done, then late is still better than not at all.

Filling out the FAFSA is a lot like doing your taxes. If your family has always paid someone to prepare your taxes and never really paid attention to the result, you might have some trouble with the terminology. Follow the instructions, and you should be fine. Unless you have really complicated business finances, you should be able to complete the form in a couple of hours.

When you are filling out the forms, be careful to avoid these common mistakes:

- Do not leave any blanks. If the question does not apply to your situation, put 0.

- Include in your untaxed income, any Earned Income Credit you received, or retirement fund contributions you made.

- Be sure to answer the questions about your parents' education. If you are a first-generation college student, you might qualify for a state grant.

- Always answer "yes" when asked about the different kinds of aid you are interested in, even if you are not. Answering "no" is not going to get more grant money, and it may stop you from getting something you may later need, like a work-study program or loans. You do not have to accept any of these when you answer "yes", but answering "no" will not leave you any options to change your mind.

- You will be asked a question about which federal income tax form you filed — 1040, 1040A, or 1040EZ. What this question is actually asking is which form you are eligible to file, which can make a difference in the amount of aid you will receive. So put 1040A or 1040EZ, unless you had no choice but file the 1040.

- Do not skip worksheets A, B, and C, which appear at the end of the application.

Double-check everything, and, as always, print or keep a copy. The first one is the hard one. The Renewal FAFSA, which you will complete in subsequent years, mostly involves putting in any changes to your income and expenses.

What Parents Can Do

There are several strategies for getting the most money you can from the financial aid process. When you file your taxes, you or your tax preparer look for deductions and strategies to reduce your tax burden. You should follow the same strategy on the FAFSA. The rules and regulations apply the same way to everyone, so it is definitely within the realm of fairness for you to follow every avenue the law allows to increase the amount of aid you can receive.

A word of caution: Do not cheat. The temptation may be great, but so are the penalties. You could be fined as much as $20,000 and face up to five years in prison. Keep in mind that colleges are required to verify the FAFSA applications of at least 30 percent of their students, and many schools verify a much higher percentage. If you are chosen for verification, you will be required to produce the documents that you used to complete the form. The chance of verification is another reason to keep copies of everything.

If you feel that a strategy you are considering might be illegal or makes you feel uneasy, feel free to talk with a financial aid administrator. They have years of experience at this and have seen it all. Their job is to help you, and they can offer sound advice to help you maximize your eligibility. You can also call FAFSA directly with questions-1-800-4FED-AID (1-800-433-3243).

There may not be a single strategy that will automatically get you where you want to be. The best thing to do is to test different strategies against your situation and decide which one(s) is going to give you the best result.

The basic idea for maximizing benefits is to reduce income, reduce included assets like savings accounts, and take advantage of the difference between how income and assets of parents and students are computed.

If both you and your parents have money in savings accounts, your money should go toward college expenses first. Student assets are counted at a higher percentage than parent's assets, so when your savings have been used up, you will actually be eligible for more aid than if your parents' money was used first.

If your parents are planning to use some of their savings to make a major purchase in the next couple of years, make it now. Putting a down payment on a new car, buying a new refrigerator, remodeling the kitchen, or any approaching payments can actually pay off by reducing your savings assets now, rather than in your junior or senior year of college. Spending money to save money sounds crazy, but remember that this is a numbers game, and you have to use the rules to your advantage if you want to win. Also, if there is money in your savings account that will be used soon for other bills, you do not have to include that portion.

Many people receive an end-of-year bonus in December. You can ask your boss if you can defer it until after Jan. 1. That will keep it off this year's books and result in a larger aid package. You will have to declare it on the second year's FAFSA, but the college will have planned to set aside the first year's aid for all four years. In other words, you might end up with a larger package for all four years instead of just the first.

Avoid capital gains. If you have property that you are planning to sell, put it off until after the final FAFSA has been filed away during the student's junior year. Selling property turns an asset into income, which is counted at a higher rate and reduces your aid.

Divorced parents

How divorce is going to affect a student's financial aid opportunities depends on several factors. Divorce can be ugly, and bitterness can creep into the financial aid process. There are cases where one parent has refused to fill out the FAFSA form. If the marriage is in the process of breaking up at the same time that you are trying to get the aid application together, life can get especially tough.

Divorce and separation can lead to a variety of complicated family relationships, but the financial aid process focuses on you and whose house you are living in. "Custodial parent" is the key concept for aid purposes, and it means the parent that you live with for more than half of the year. It makes no difference who has legal custody or who is responsible for paying child support.

For example, if Jimmy's parents divorced two years ago and he lives with his father, then Dad is the custodial parent, and they have a family of two persons. Only Dad's income and assets will be considered, although Mom may have to file a FAFSA. If Dad remarries, even if it is the day he fills out the FAFSA form, there is now a family of three and both Dad and his new wife's income and assets will have to be included on the FAFSA, along with any children the new wife brings to the family. When those children need financial aid, their new stepfather's income and assets will be considered along with their mom's assets.

This scenario is straightforward, but things can get confusing very quickly. Parents are accustomed to thinking of the children who live with them in terms of tax exemptions, which are based not only on where the child lives but on who provides their support or who was granted the exemption by court order. Financial aid does not work that way. If a stepchild lives in your house but receives more than 50 percent of his support from an ex-spouse, you cannot claim that child as a tax exemption, but he or she is part of your household for financial aid purposes. That child's biological parent would have to claim any child support received as untaxed income. What counts is where the child physically spends most of his or her time.

Another difference between financial aid rules and IRS rules is that a child can be a tax exemption for only one person but can be counted as part of more than one household for financial aid purposes. Let us say that Jack and Jill have a son named William. Jack and Jill get divorced, and as part of the agreement William lives with Jill, but Jack provides more than 50 percent of his support. Jack remarries, and his new wife has a daughter the same age as William. They are both ready for college. Jack gets to claim his new daughter, as well as his son for whom he is providing support, as part of his household. His new daughter will get more financial aid because Jack will have two children in college. When William's mother fills out his FAFSA, she also gets to claim William as part of her household. Even though she does not provide more than 50 percent of his support, she is the custodial parent. Therefore, William is counted as being in two households for aid purposes.

If your parents have shared custody and each contributes 50 percent of your support then you can actually use the parent who makes the least, just do not forget to include any stepparents' income as well.

The PROFILE

Many private schools require the PROFILE form as a supplement to the FAFSA. Unlike the FAFSA, you have to register for the PROFILE form on the College Board's website (**www.collegeboard.com**) and pay a $25 processing fee for the first school or scholarship and an additional $16 for each school that you want to send the completed form to. You need to be sure which schools you want to apply to and whether they require this form to save yourself some headaches and money.

The PROFILE covers much of the same ground as the FAFSA, but the College Board also maintains a database of questions that are used by individual schools to gather more detail than the FAFSA. For example, PROFILE filers have to produce three years of income information instead of one and also have to provide additional information about home ownership. On the positive side, the PROFILE can allow for more expenses than the FAFSA form.

When you register and choose the schools that will receive the form, the website automatically brings up these school-specific questions for you and takes care of delivering the answers to the right school.

If you are filing the FAFSA, the PROFILE, and perhaps additional school-specific forms, you need to make sure that you have been consistent across the forms. Some private colleges will want to know both parents' income, even if they are divorced. Sometimes this may be difficult to get, but unless the circumstances are unusual (in which hopefully the college agrees with you about the reason for not getting the information), you will have to find a way.

The Student Aid Report (SAR)

Now that you have submitted all the forms (after making copies of everything), it is time to relax and wait a few weeks. It takes usually two weeks to get your results (SAR) when filing online, but it will take three to six weeks to get your SAR via regular mail. In either case, this is an important document and you should make sure that you keep a copy along with all of the other forms you have accumulated to this point.

Check the SAR to make sure that the numbers are accurate and that it has been sent to the correct schools. If you have decided to apply to additional schools, contact the financial aid office at those schools for further instructions.

The SAR will give you two important pieces of information. The first is whether you are eligible for the Pell Grant, which is free money the government gives to low-income students. This can be as much as $5,775 per year.

The second piece of information the SAR gives you is your Expected Family Contribution (EFC). This is the SAT score of financial aid. Except that in this case, the lower the number, the more aid you are going to get.

If your EFC is way out of line with what you can actually pay, you can ask the financial aid office for a professional judgment, which is a review of your EFC owing to special circumstances. If you have unusually high medical bills, for example, your financial aid officer may reduce your

EFC. An important consideration when going this route is to do it before you actually commit to the school. The financial aid officer may be more cooperative if more aid will ensure that you attend that school.

Be aware, however, that a professional judgment in your favor is not necessarily going to result in more free money. More likely, your offer of loans is going to increase. But if there is a recent change of income for some reason, such as divorce, death, or loss of job, then the college can also increase your grant money.

The Offers

The college's financial aid offer usually arrives along with an acceptance letter. The offer will most likely contain a combination of several components: grants, loans, and work-study. Just remember, their definition of financial "awards" isn't usually the normal meaning of the word "awards." It usually includes loans (that you have to repay) and work-study money (which until you actually have a job at the college and work those hours, you will not receive).

The financial aid officer who completes your package goes about it in this manner. First, he or she will calculate the cost of attendance, taking into consideration whether you are a residential or commuter student. Your EFC is subtracted from this figure, along with any federal or state grants. Scholarships and other outside funding are also subtracted.

That usually leaves some costs, referred to as the remaining financial need (RFN). This need is met with federal loans and federal work-study, which in financial aid terms is referred to as self-help because it is a contribution on top of the EFC. Colleges try to level out the self-help amounts because they have the most direct impact on families. This need, if extreme, can also be a special grant for very low incomes.

When financial aid officers are calculating all of these components for an individual student, they look at eligibility, need, and merit. Eligibility for loans and grants is usually straightforward. Either you meet the financial criteria, or you do not. Need can be more subjective. Colleges have a certain amount of grant money available, and they can choose to give the bulk of it to the more unfortunate students or distribute it among most of the student population. This choice could have a big impact on whether you receive loans or grants, and it is why aid offers can vary greatly from school to school.

Merit aid is subjective and reflects the needs and values of the school. The school controls this money, so they can decide if they want to use it to attract students with special abilities in athletics, music, academics, or drama or even just focus on STEM (science, technology, engineering, mathematic) majors. Some schools have dropped merit aid entirely and give out money based solely on need. The more selective the school, the less likely they are to hand out merit aid because they have less need to attract talented students.

Financial aid officers take care to address each individual student's needs with all of this in mind. But since schools operate with different goals and values in mind, offers from different schools will vary even though they are working with the same basic raw material.

Comparing offers

Make a chart that lists the amounts of aid you are going to receive, then make another chart that compares loan amounts and your own contributions. For instance, it sounds great if a school offers you $20,000 in aid for the year, but it might not be a good deal if you are left with $10,000 in loans to repay and $6,000 to pay out of pocket. Similarly, a school that offers you only $12,000 in aid but leaves you with a smaller amount of loans and money you have to pay yourself is a better deal. What you need to do is make a chart that lists the amounts of aid you are going to receive, then make another chart that compares loan amounts and your own contributions. These are the important numbers at this point.

It should be easy to see which school is the best bargain for you, but it might not be the school you choose to attend. You might decide that it is worth the extra cost to attend a more prestigious school, or you may simply be willing to pay more to attend a school that you like better or one that has your particular major. The choice is ultimately up to you.

Before you sign on the dotted line, there is one final step. As we have seen, the financial aid offer is partly the result of a subjective process. That means there is some room for negotiation. Financial aid officers can exercise what is called "professional judgment" to increase, or in some cases radically improve offers of aid. Do not assume, however, that the negotiations are going to work. If the financial aid package from the school you want to attend has made it easily affordable for you, then it is probably a great deal already, and you are not going to get any more. The financial aid office knows what other students are getting and is not going to listen long to whining. At the same time, if you happen to be the type of student that they really want to come to their school, they may up the offer.

If the school you want to attend has provided an unworkable package or you have received radically different financial aid offers from similar schools and the school you want is on the lower end, then it is worth it to negotiate. It is especially worthwhile if the school really wants you because of your high SAT and/or ACT scores, grade point average, or special talents. They are going to be less likely to budge if you barely made it in.

Parents: Do not go into a professional judgment interview and complain about your high credit card debt, the payments on your new boat, or the gambling debts that have left you strapped. These are problems that you created, and financial aid officers who probably do not make as much as you do are not going to have much sympathy, just as the FAFSA will not take these things into consideration.

However, there are legitimate circumstances that are not covered by the FAFSA, which can leave you with an unrealistic aid package and which the school's financial aid office can take into consideration in your case. Unusual capital gains, a recent bankruptcy, termination of a child support agreement, unusually high medical expenses, or a drop in income are legitimate reasons to ask for a review of your case.

Have a plan ready. If you or your parents are basing your argument on a particular financial situation, such as support of an elderly relative or unusually high unreimbursed business expenses, be prepared to document your case. Similarly, if your argument is based on radically different aid packages from similar schools, be prepared to show them the aid letters. They will probably ask to see them anyway. If there has been a drastic change in your life since you filed the aid forms — divorce, job loss — let the financial aid office know about it. If you make a good case and the school wants you, they will make a better offer that could save you thousands of dollars. At this point, they really do not have a lot of money left to throw your way, so even if the upgrade is small, walk away happy. Even if things are not going your way, the worst thing they can do is say no, and they cannot take back an offer they have already made. So you have nothing to lose.

When you are ready to accept, you have one decision left to make. The financial aid package is composed of several components, and you have the option of rejecting one or all of these. You may, for instance, want to reject a work-study or loan offer if you have a better way of making up the difference. Be aware, though, that rejecting any kind of aid may lessen the amount that you receive in upcoming years when you might really need it. You can always accept a loan and only use it if absolutely necessary or even save it for the final years of your education. If you do not use it, you can keep any interest earned, return it in full after you graduate, and at the same time, increase your credit standing. As for the work-study program, keep in mind that you can usually walk away from that job at any time if it does not work out for you, and it pays more than minimum wage jobs. Check out your school's regulations on this before you try it.

Some Good News

After all of this detail about how much college is going to cost you, it is time for a little good news. Paying for college offers some significant tax benefits. The rules tend to change, so you might want to consult a tax adviser.

The Hope tax credit provides up to a $2,500 tax credit for the first two years of out-of-pocket tuition and fee expenses per student. For parents with more than one student in school, this can be a major break. The key words here are out-of-pocket. There are also income limits.

The Lifetime Learning Tax Credit kicks in after your Hope eligibility is gone. This credit is for 20 percent of your qualified tuition expenses, no matter who they are for, up to $2,000. The best part is that this credit is good indefinitely, but it does have the same income limits as the Hope Scholarship.

After graduation, student loan interest that you have paid during the year is an above-the-line income, which means that it reduces your adjusted gross income. The majority of the federal loans you will receive will be in your name. But the Parent Plus loans (which is a loan made out to the parent and is paid on by the parent or by you if that is the agreement between you-while you are attending school) or private loans are usually in the parents' names. There are income limitations, so if your parents are not going to get this benefit, you might want to be sure that any student loans are in your name, or changed to your name, so you can claim the deduction. The regulations state that only the person legally obligated to repay the loan can take the deduction, regardless of who is actually making the payments. Only the person who signed the bottom line is going to get the tax benefits.

Depending on your income and your parents' income, these tax benefits can reduce your actual expenditures to zero. Keep in mind, though, that these tax goodies tend to change frequently, so keep an eye out at tax time for any changes.

Upcoming FAFSA Changes

Besides creating a user name and password in place of a PIN, there are two other major changes for the 2017-2018 school year with the FAFSA: First, you will be able to apply in October of 2016 (instead of January of 2017). Second, FAFSA can collect income information from an earlier year. This will help the student estimate the amount of aid that they will receive earlier.

Wrapping It Up

The financial aid process can be the most daunting task when preparing for college. It is complicated and confusing at times, and frustrating at others. But it must be done, and the payoff makes it worth all of the work. Like college itself, you will need to do your research and study hard. You can make the financial aid process work for you so that you can afford college. With the right tools and some hard work, your application and aid letters will deliver the goods right to your door.

The FAFSA, although important, is only a part of the process of getting money for college. In the next chapters, you will discover how scholarships, grants, and work opportunities offer excellent ways of paying for college. You can combine these with your financial aid package, or add to it. Unbelievably, we are only just getting started.

Chapter 4

Grants

Before we consider loan money that you borrow and pay back, let us explore money you do not have to pay back: grants. Grants are a great way to cut the costs of college, and grant money does not have to be returned. While scholarships are generally based on performance, grants are often (but not always) based on need. Grants can range from $100 to covering full tuition costs at a four-year college or university. They can be a great supplement to your financing for college, as it is that much less that you have to borrow or get from another source. Plus, once you finish college, it will be that much less you have to pay back. After all, loan payments can be a hefty check to write every month for years on end. Even with the low-interest rate loans students have access to, the amount of the original loan can be doubled by the time you pay them off. A monthly payment for a student loan can easily reach the $200 to $500 per month range, so it is in your best interest to take advantage of all the free money that you can receive. Most students end up wishing they had borrowed less, as the payments can be very hard to manage. Although loans make it possible for many to attend school, they still have to be paid back. Your goal should be to keep your debt down to a minimum, and one way to do it is to take advantage of grants. Apply for as many as you can.

So, how do you find out about grants? A good place to start is with the financial aid office of the college that you will be attending. The financial aid office is familiar with both state and federal grants that are available to students. Most states have grants for their residents attending state-funded schools, and you should contact your state's Department of Education to find out if there are any you may be eligible for. There are also websites that can help you track down grants that may be available from private sources, which we will explore shortly. Private sources may be companies that are using grants for college as public relations tools (while utilizing the possible tax deduction), or they may be offered by a private individual that is trying to assist certain kinds of students with certain kinds of needs. For instance, the grant may be designed for American Indian students who are planning to use their studies to help on a reservation. They may be specific, such as a grant designed for single mothers studying dentistry, or they may be broad, such as art students who are working on their BFA degree at a specific art college.

If you look hard enough, you will certainly find a grant for which you are qualified to apply. A great site you can try is **www.fastweb.com**. This is a popular site that many college financial aid offices recommend as a supplemental source to find and apply for private grants and other funding, such as scholarships. According to Fastweb, they are "recommended by over 15,500 high schools and 3,500 colleges." Fastweb users answer a detailed questionnaire, and the data then generates possibilities for scholarships, grants, internships, and more. This saves you time and effort, as the information given to you is for suitable possibilities, meaning money for which you are qualified to apply. However, you can search the whole database if you desire. Just remember to be patient when searching, as they will also pull up results where only one thing matches your qualifications, such as a grant for a fellowship in your major for graduate students, which you would be ineligible for as an undergraduate, or a grant for education majors who live in New York, even though you live in Florida. Many times one word may match you to a grant or scholarship that you are really not eligible for. You will have to sift through all of the matches, but do not get discouraged, as there should still be something for you to apply to.

Although many of the available grants are given out according to financial need, some grants are merit-based, while others are designed to promote a particular field of study or to encourage students to attend private schools. They may be even be based on ethnicity, religion, or association. For instance, you may find a grant that is specifically designed for those who are studying art at a private college or a grant created for those who plan on working in human services. You might discover grants that require a high GPA for a particular field of study, such as math or science. There are plenty of private grants out there, and you may be qualified for more than one. Private grants can be used in addition to government grants, both of which we will go over in more detail shortly.

Grants, whether private or government-funded, are created to help you reduce the costs of college. They are not designed to be used for a vacation to Bermuda, a new stereo system for your dorm room, a down payment on a new vehicle, or new clothing for your wardrobe. They are specifically intended to be used for tuition, books, and other school supplies. Many grants pay the funds to the school directly, so the money never reaches your hands. If you drop out of school, you might have to pay a portion of that financial aid back (especially if the aid is through the federal government), depending on the date. You will no longer be able to continue with the work-study program if you are a part of that either.

As with all your financial planning for college, be sure to apply for grant money early. Many grant funds are limited. Every deadline differs, but it is generally a good idea to get all of your financial applications in by Feb. 15.

Federal Grants

Federal grants are, by definition, an award of financial assistance from a federal agency. As presented in Chapter 3, one of the first steps you will want to take when applying for a federal grant is to fill out the Free Application for Federal Student Aid, or FAFSA form. Remember, it is now preferred for you to apply online, but you should still be able to find them at the college financial aid offices, at www.fafsa.ed.gov, or by calling the Federal Student Aid, an office of the U.S. Department of Education, at 1-800-4-FED-AID (1-800-433-3243). Again, make sure you file the form as early as possible, as some grants have limited funds for the year.

Pell Grants

The name "Pell Grant" is in honor of Senator Claiborne Pell from Rhode Island. He was a long-time advocate of federal funding for higher education. Pell Grants provide more than 90 percent of all federal grant money (veterans' benefits excluded). They are awarded to undergraduates who have not yet received a bachelor's degree. Pell Grants are based on the financial needs of the applicant, taking into consideration the size of the student's household, the amount of their yearly income, and depending on the college, the cost of tuition at the school the student has chosen. This information is based on what you submit in the Free Application for Federal Student Aid (FAFSA), as described in Chapter 3. The maximum amount of a Pell Grant per award year has for the 2015-2016 year has been raised to $5,775 although this amount is set every year depending on the funding. The amount of the grant is also determined by the student's cost of attending school and whether the student will be a full-time or part-time student. A student's eligibility is determined by the Expected Family Contribution (EFC), the amount that you and your family are expected to pay out of pocket for your education.

To qualify for the Pell Grant, you need to have an EFC less than $5,775. While it is possible to receive a Pell Grant if your family's household income is $75,000 or more, most recipients' household income is under $50,000. According to Fastweb data, "95.9% of Pell Grant recipients in 2007-08 had an adjusted gross income (AGI) of $50,000 or less, 3-5% had an AGI of $75,000 to $100,000." All of this depends on a variety of factors beyond AGI, such as the number of people in college at the time. The lower the EFC, the more likely you are to receive the grant. You may receive the Pell Grant for every year that you work toward your bachelor's degree in education, as there is no limit on the number of times you receive it as long as you qualify. However, you may only receive one Pell Grant per year, although the funds received are paid by semesters.

Some of the eligibility requirements to receive a Pell Grant include:

- You must demonstrate a financial need by submitting a Free Application for Federal Student Aid (FAFSA).
- You must be a U.S. citizen or an eligible noncitizen.
- You must have a high school diploma or a GED.
- You must not have defaulted on any student loans.
- You must have a valid Social Security Number.
- You must be enrolled in an eligible postsecondary school.
- You must be working toward a first undergraduate degree or teaching credential.
- Male applicants must have registered for the Selective Service, if they are between the ages of 18 and 25.
- Satisfactory academic progress must be maintained.
- You must certify that the funds will be used only for educational purposes.
- The following people are ineligible to receive a Pell Grant:
- Those who owe a refund on a grant made by a federal student aid program under Title IV of the Higher Education Act.
- Those who default on a Title IV loan.
- Those who are incarcerated.
- Those who have been convicted of possessing or selling illegal drugs.

Things to keep in mind with a Pell Grant are that not every school participates in the federal grant program. Some degree programs are ineligible, you may receive only one Pell Grant in an award year, and you may not receive Pell Grant funds from more than one school at a time. You may also receive a Pell Grant for every academic year until you receive a bachelor's degree, and the grant can be transferred to another school if you change schools within an aid year. Always ask your college's financial aid office about a Pell Grant, even if you think you may not be eligible.

There are times when special circumstances may come into play when considering the amount that you will receive. The special circumstance may include something like a drastic change in income or a student who incurred major medical expenses that are not covered by insurance policies. Also, if you have disability-related expenses, such as wheelchairs, interpreters, and personal attendants, they can be used to help enhance your award amount. Your school's financial aid office can assist with making a case for special circumstances.

The Pell Grant has requirements regarding residency, starting with the fact you must be able to live and attend school legally in the United States as a U.S. citizen, a U.S. national, or an eligible noncitizen.

Eligible noncitizens would include those who are:

- U.S. permanent residents (Alien Registration Card or I-551)
- Conditional permanent residents (I-551C Card)
- Refugees, asylum grantees, or parolees
- Cuban-Haitian entrants with Arrival Departure Records (I-94) from the Immigration and Naturalization Service (INS).

If you are collecting Social Security (SSI), you may still receive the Pell Grant without jeopardizing your SSI eligibility. Unlike other money you might receive, grants are not considered income or assets if they are used for school purposes, such as tuition, fees, or other education expenses. The same goes if you are receiving Social Security Disability Insurance (SSDI.): You may still receive the Pell Grant while collecting SSDI.

If you are collecting Social Security due to a disability, you might want to consider a Plan for Achieving Self-Support (PASS). A PASS will allow you to set aside otherwise countable income and/or resources for a specific period in order to achieve a work goal. According to the Social Security Administration, "Under SSI rules, any income that you have may reduce your SSI payment. But, if you have an approved plan, you can use that income to pay for the items you need to reach your work goal." A PASS can be used for tuition, books, or other supplies needed to attend school. You must have the PASS plan approved first. You can find out more by calling the Social Security Administration at 1-800-772-1213 or by visiting **www.ssa.gov**.

Academic Competitiveness Grant and National SMART Grants

According to the U.S. Department of Education, two grants are available to those that are studying topics in math, science, technology, engineering, and critical foreign languages: The Academic Competitiveness Grant (ACG) and National Science and Mathematics Access to Retain Talent (National SMART Grant) Programs. These are performance-based and are awarded to those who have demonstrated a financial need.

If you are in your first or second academic year of college, you may be eligible for the Academic Competitiveness Grant and receive up to $750 for the first year of study and up to $1,300 for the second year. During your third and fourth academic years, you may be eligible for a National SMART Grant and receive up to $4,000 for each year of study.

Requirements for Academic Competitiveness Grant and National SMART Grants are, for each year of study:

- You must be a U.S. citizen.
- You must be attending school full-time in a four-year degree-granting institution.
- You must be eligible to receive a Pell Grant.
- You must meet other eligibility requirements related to — depending on your year in school — completing a rigorous

high school curriculum; majoring in mathematics, science, or selected foreign languages; and maintaining a required minimum grade point average (GPA).

Keep in mind that only certain learning institutions participate in the program. If you are eligible to receive either grant, the funds may go directly to your student account at the school, or the funds may be paid directly to you. Or it may be a combination of both — some funds go in your school account, and the rest are given to you. For more information, ask your financial aid office at your high school or college, or visit the U.S. Department of Education at: **https://studentaid.ed.gov/sa** or call the Federal Student Aid Information Center (FSAIC) 1-800-4-FED-AID (1-800-433-3243).

Supplemental Educational Opportunity Grants

Other federal grants that are need-based are the Federal Supplemental Education Opportunity Grants (FSEOG). FSEO grants range from $100 to $4,000 and are distributed at least once per term (semester, trimester, or quarter) and at least twice per academic year.

The grants are designed for undergraduates or vocational students who are enrolled in school at least half-time, and are pursuing their first bachelor's degree and have exceptional financial need. Students who are already receiving a Pell Grant are given priority to receive a FSEOG. Determination is made by Expected Family Contribution (EFC) score, which was determined on their financial aid application, and they are awarded to the less fortunate students first. But unlike a Pell Grant, there is a possibility that a student awarded a FSEOG will not receive the money. Colleges receive a limited amount of funding for the program each year. Therefore, they can only give the grant to a certain number of students per year. Some schools do not participate in the program. Check with your school's financial aid office for more details about the FSEOG.

Leveraging Educational Assistance Partnership (LEAP)

The Leveraging Educational Assistance Partnership is also known as the "LEAP Program." Instead of providing grants directly to students, the program provides grants to states in order to help them provide their own need-based grants and community service work-study assistance. The states each apply for this federal program, and they administer it under a single state agency. The agency must follow certain criteria. Both undergraduate and graduate students, who must demonstrate extreme financial need, may apply for the program in the state that they are residents. Some of the eligibility requirements for the program are:

- You must demonstrate financial need.
- You must be eligible to receive the Pell Grant.
- You must be a U.S. citizen or an eligible noncitizen.
- You must not have defaulted on any student loans.
- Male applicants must have registered for the Selective Service.
- Satisfactory academic progress must be maintained.

Other stipulations may be required. Check with your state's human services department or Department of Education, or ask your school's financial aid office to help point you in the right direction.

In addition to the LEAP Program, there is the SLEAP Program, which is available to states that participate in the LEAP Program. According to the U.S. Department of Education, "The SLEAP Program assists states in providing student aid programs for eligible students pursuing their postsecondary education and who have substantial financial need. The student aid programs can be in the form of supplemental grants, supplemental community service work-study employment, or merit and academic achievement or critical career scholarships." Both undergraduate and graduate students with financial needs may apply to their residential state.

For more information, visit **www.ed.gov**, call the Federal Student Aid Information Center at 800-433-3243 or 800- 4FED-AID, or ask your school's financial aid office.

Federal Agency Grants

Federal agency grants are grants that come from places like the National Endowment for the Arts, an independent federal agency. Federal agency grants are awarded for reasons other than education, such as projects and research. Every federal agency that offers grants has its own set of eligibility requirements, all depending on the type of grant and the agency itself. One of the best resources to check for federal agency grants is www.grants.gov. There are 26 federal grant-making agencies available through the site that you can link to and apply for grants with. There are over 1,000 Federal agency grants available, with approximately $400 billion in annual awards, some of which are for educational purposes or can be used to help fund education. Grants are designed for everyone, including small businesses, organizations, and individuals, all of which you can easily research on the site. According to Grants.gov, the federal agencies that provide grants include:

- **Agency for International Development:** An independent federal government agency that provides economic and humanitarian assistance in more than 100 countries.

- **Corporation for National and Community Service:**
  The nation's largest grant-maker supporting service
  and volunteering.

- **Department of Agriculture:** Serves all Americans through
  anti-hunger efforts, stewardship of nearly 200 million acres of
  national forest and rangelands, and through product safety and
  conservation efforts.

- **Department of Commerce:** Fosters and promotes the nation's
  economic development and technological advancement
  through vigilance in international trade policy, domestic
  business policy and growth, and promoting economic progress
  at all levels.

- **Department of Defense:** Provides the military forces needed
  to deter war and protect the security of the United States,
  including peacekeeping, war-fighting efforts, evacuation, and
  humanitarian causes.

- **Department of Education:** Ensures equal access to education
  and promotes educational excellence through coordination,
  management, and accountability in federal education programs.

- **Department of Energy:** Advances national, economic, and
  energy security in the U.S.; promotes scientific and technological
  innovation in support of that goal; and ensures environmental
  cleanup of the national nuclear weapons complex.

- **Department of Health and Human Services:** The federal
  government's principal agency for protecting the health of all
  Americans and providing essential human services, especially to
  those who are least able to help themselves.

- **Department of Homeland Security:** Has three primary missions: Prevent terrorist attacks within the United States, reduce America's vulnerability to terrorism, and minimize the damage from potential attacks and natural disasters.

- **Department of Housing and Urban Development:** Their mission is to increase homeownership, support community development, and increase access to affordable housing free from discrimination.

- **Department of the Interior:** Protects and provides access to the Nation's natural and cultural heritage, including responsibilities to Indian tribes and island communities.

- **Department of Justice:** Enforces the law and defends the interest of the United States, ensuring public safety against threats foreign and domestic; provides federal leadership in preventing and controlling crime; seeks just punishment for those guilty of unlawful pursuits; and ensures fair and impartial administration of justice for all Americans.

- **Department of Labor:** Fosters and promotes the welfare of job seekers, wage earners, and retirees by improving their working conditions, advancing their opportunities, protecting their retirement and health benefits, and generally protecting worker rights and monitoring national economic measures.

- **Department of State:** Strives to create a more secure, democratic, and prosperous world for the benefit of the American people and the international community.

- **Department of Transportation:** Their mission is to ensure fast, safe, efficient, accessible, and convenient transportation that meets vital national interests and enhances the quality of life of the American people, today and into the future.

- **Department of the Treasury:** A steward of United States economic and financial systems, they promote conditions for prosperity and stability in the U.S., and encourage prosperity and stability in the rest of the world.

- **Department of Veterans Affairs:** Strives for excellence in patient care and veteran's benefits for its constituents through high quality, prompt, and seamless service to United States veterans.

- **Environmental Protection Agency:** Their mission is to protect human health and the environment.

- **Institute of Museum and Library Services:** The primary source of federal support for the nation's 122,000 libraries and 17,500 museums.

- **National Aeronautics and Space Administration:** Serves as the nation's forefront of such exploration and continues to pioneer in aeronautics, exploration systems, science, and space operations.

- **National Archives and Records Administration:** Enables people to inspect the record of what the federal government has done, enables officials and agencies to review their actions, and helps citizens hold them accountable.

- **National Endowment for the Arts:** A public agency dedicated to supporting excellence in the arts; bringing the arts to all Americans and providing leadership in arts education.

- **National Endowment for the Humanities:** An independent grant-making agency of the United States government dedicated to supporting research, education, preservation, and public programs in the humanities.

- **National Science Foundation:** An independent federal agency created to promote the progress of science, to advance the national health, prosperity, and welfare, and to secure the national defense.

- **Small Business Administration:** Maintains and strengthens the nation's economy by aiding, counseling, assisting, and protecting the interests of small businesses and by helping families and businesses recover from national disasters.

- **Social Security Administration:** Advances the economic security of the nation's people through compassionate and vigilant leadership in shaping and managing America's Social Security programs.

State Grants

Most states have grant programs to assist with the costs of college. However, like many grants they are often need-based. Some other types of state grants are designed to assist with certain degree programs, such as high-need fields, like teaching, nursing, or STEM majors. Other types include grants for women, minorities, students with disabilities, foster care youth, or veterans. Each state varies and you need to thoroughly look into the grants available to you through yours. Keep in mind that some states have signed reciprocity agreements with other states to offer need-based grant programs to out-of-state undergraduates. This is something to consider if you are a resident in a state other than where you are attending college. Also, remember that the yearly budget for grants can change. One year there may be more funds allocated for grants, meaning more students will receive grant money or that the money each student will receive will vary. Generally, the first step is to complete your FAFSA, as presented in Chapter 3.

Just to give you an idea what state grants are available, let us look at a few.

Alabama residents can apply for the Alabama Student Assistance Program, a state/federal aid program designed for undergraduate students. Awards range from $300 to $5,000 per year. For more information, call the Alabama Commission of Higher Education at (334) 242-1998, visit **www.ache.state.al.us**, or check with your school's financial aid office.

Cal Grants are offered through the California Student Aid Commission. They are designed to help students that are pursuing an undergraduate associate's degree, bachelor's degree, or an occupational training program at any qualifying California college, university, or career or technical school. The grants assist low- to middle-income students, who are attending private or public college and pursuing vocational or career training. With a Cal Grant, you can receive up to $12,240 a year (dependent upon the type of college) to help pay for college expenses. Each grant has certain requirements that must be met, like maintaining a certain GPA. To find out more about Cal Grants, visit the California Student Aid Commission at **www.csac.ca.gov**, call 888-CA GRANT (224-7268), or ask your financial aid office more information.

Qualified Colorado residents can take advantage of the Colorado National Guard Tuition Assistance Program and get up to 100 percent of tuition costs paid at state-supported institutions. For more information, contact a National Guard recruiter or the state tuition assistance office at (303) 677-8913. You can also call the Colorado Department of Education at 303-866-2723, or visit **http://highered.colorado.gov** for information on more state aid.

In Florida, residents can apply for the Florida Bright Futures Scholarship Program, a program that establishes three lottery-funded scholarships to reward high school graduates for academic achievement. Or they can apply for other funds, such as the José Martí Scholarship Challenge Grant Fund. This need-based merit award is designed for eligible students of Hispanic origin who will attend Florida public or eligible private institutions and are enrolled in a minimum of 12 credit hours for undergraduate study or nine credit hours for graduate study. Students must apply during their senior year of high school. There are other grants as well, including the First Generation Grant, the Florida Fund for Minority Teachers, the Florida Resident Access Grant, Rosewood Family Grant, and others. (For more information, contact the Florida Department of Education's Office of Student Financial Assistance at 888-827-2004, visit **www.floridastudentfinancialaid.org**, or check with your school's financial aid office.)

Georgia residents can apply for the Georgia Tuition Equalization Grant Program that was designed to assist undergraduate students with attending eligible private colleges in Georgia. The amount of the award is $300 per quarter or $450 per semester for up to four quarters or three semesters per year. For more information, visit the Georgia Student Finance Commission at **http://gacollege411.org**, or email **support@ GAcollege411.org**.

Illinois offers a Grant Program for Dependents of Police or Fire Officers for those who are working on undergraduate and graduate degrees at approved Illinois colleges. According to the State of Illinois' site **www. isac.org**, "If you are the spouse or child of an Illinois police or fire officer who was killed or became at least 90 percent disabled in the line of duty, you may be eligible for the Grant Program for Dependents of Police or Fire Officers." If eligible, you may receive the equivalent amount of eight semesters or 12 quarters of assistance. There are also several more grants, such as the Illinois National Guard Grant, the Monetary Award Program, and others. Find out more at **www.isac.org**, call the Illinois Student Assistance Commission at 800-899-ISAC (4722), or check your school's financial aid office.

In Maryland (and other states as well), doctoral students can apply for the Southern Regional Education Board (SREB) Doctoral Scholars Program. According to the Maryland Higher Education Commission "[The Program] is designed to increase the number of minority faculty in the 16-state SREB region by encouraging ethnic minorities to pursue doctoral degrees and become college-level teachers." The Doctoral Scholars Program Award is quite generous as it offers five years of support, starting with a waiver of tuition and fees during the first three years and awarding on an individual basis in the final two years. For application information, visit the SREB website at **www.sreb.org**. For more information about the Southern Regional Education Board (SREB)

Doctoral Scholars Program, contact the Maryland Higher Education Commission at (410) 260-4500, 800-974-0203, or visit **www.mhec. state.md.us**.

New York residents can take advantage of the Tuition Assistance Program (TAP). It is New York's largest grant program and is based on income or your family's New York State net taxable income. If you are eligible for a TAP grant you can receive up to $5,165 per year at an approved school. Part-time students are eligible for a part-time TAP. You can find out more and apply for TAP at the New York State Higher Education Services Corporation website **www.hesc.ny.gov**, call (888) NYSHESC, or ask your financial aid office more information.

In North Dakota, residents can take advantage of the North Dakota Academic Scholarship. Awards are designed for those who are earning their undergraduate degree and who attend North Dakota's public, private (not-for-profit), and tribal colleges. The awards range up to $6,000 total. For more information on this and other grants, call the North Dakota University System at 701-328-2960, visit **www.ndus.edu**, or check with your school's financial aid office.

North Carolina residents can take advantage of several grant opportunities, including the NC Community College Grant & Loan Program, which is designed for students who are enrolled at North Carolina community colleges. According to the College Foundation of North Carolina, "Eligibility is determined based on the same criteria as the Federal Pell Grant; students not eligible for the Federal Pell Grant may be considered for the grant based on their estimated family contribution as determined on the Student Aid Report. Students who have earned the baccalaureate (4 year) college degree are ineligible." The amount of the grant varies according to information that is generated from the Pell Grant application. For more information, call the College Foundation of North Carolina at 888-234-6400 (toll free), visit **www.cfnc.org**, or check with your school's financial aid office.

In Ohio, residents can take advantage of the Ohio College Opportunity Grant (OCOG), a need-based tuition assistance for low- to moderate-income families. This is based on total family income and the Expected Family contribution (EFC) from FAFSA. For more information on this and other grants, contact the Ohio Board of Regents at 888-833-1133, visit **www.ohiohighered.org/ocog**, or check with your school's financial aid office.

Rhode Island residents can visit riheaa.org for information on several scholarships and grants for their residents, including the Academic Promise Program, the RI Scholar Recognition, and other programs. For more information, contact the Rhode Island Higher Education Assistance Authority at 401-736-1100 or 800-922-9855.

If you are a Texas resident who has demonstrated a financial need (and other academic requirements), you can take advantage of the Tuition Equalization Grant Program (TEG) and receive up to $3,346 per school year. Students who have demonstrated an exceptional financial need may receive up to $5,046 in a given year. To find out more about this grant and others, ask your school's financial aid office, visit College for Texans at **www.collegeforalltexans.com**, call the Texas Higher Education Coordinating Board's Division of Student Services at 800-242-3062 (outside the Austin area) or at 512-427-6340 (in the Austin area), or check with your school's financial aid office.

Utah offers the Utah Centennial Opportunity Program for Education (UCOPE) Grant for qualified undergraduate residents who are attending schools in Utah. UCOPE grants are funded by the state, but not all Utah schools offer UCOPE grants. For more information on this and other Utah state grants, call the Utah Higher Education Assistance

Authority at 800-418-2551, visit **www.uheaa.org**, or check with your school's financial aid office.

Vermont residents enrolled in an undergraduate degree or certificate program who will be attending college full-time and do not already have a bachelor's degree are eligible to apply for a Vermont Incentive Grant. Residents attending the University of Vermont College of Medicine or enrolled in a Doctor of Veterinary medicine program are also eligible to apply. The awards are based on financial need, and the amount is based on funding available. They can be used at schools either within Vermont or out of state. Vermont Part-Time Grants are also available to those who are enrolled in an undergraduate degree or certificate program and who will be attending less than full-time (unless they are attending the University of Vermont College of Medicine or enrolled in a doctor of veterinary medicine program). The grants are based on financial need. Students must be taking fewer than 12 credits per semester and not have already received a bachelor's degree. The amount of each award varies, depending on credit hours. For more information on these and other grants, call Vermont Student Assistance at 800-882-4166 or 802-654-3750, visit **www.vsac.org**, or check with your school's financial aid office.

Washington State also offers its residents a state grant program, the State Need Grant (SNG). This program helps low income undergraduate students and has to be used at an eligible Washington institution. The amounts vary. Washington State also offers the Educational Opportunity Grant (EOG). This program was designed to help low-income adults train for high-wage, high-demand careers. The amount can pay up to 45 credits within three years. It also may cover tuition and fees and up to $1,000 yearly for supplies and books. Certain eligibility requirements apply. To find out more about these and more grants, contact the Washington Higher Education Coordinating Board at 360-596-4803, or check with your school's financial aid office.

Wisconsin has several grant programs available to qualified resident students, including the Indian Student Assistance Grant. This grant was designed for undergraduate or graduate students who are at least 25 percent Native American and are enrolled in degree or certificate programs at the University of Wisconsin, Wisconsin Technical College, independent colleges and universities, tribal colleges, or proprietary institutions based in Wisconsin. The grant is based on financial need, ranges from $250 to $1,100, and has a limit of 10 semesters of eligibility. Students must be enrolled at least part-time (including less than half-time). Minority students (African-American, American Indian, Hispanic, or Southeast Asian from Laos, Cambodia, or Vietnam) may apply for the Minority Undergraduate Retention Grant. Grants are based on financial need with a maximum grant of $2,500 per year for up to eight semesters or 12 quarters. For more information, contact the State of Wisconsin Higher Educational Aids Board at 608-267-2206, visit **www.heab.state.wi.us**, or check with your school's financial aid office.

As you can see, many states offer a wide range of grants designed for assistance with higher education. This list was created to show examples of what is available and is by no means all-inclusive. It is subject to change yearly, depending on the availability of funds. For more information about your state's grants, inquire with your state's Department of Education, or ask your college financial aid office. The Online Education Database, **http://oedb.org**, also has a search engine for state grants, as well as categories such as minority college grants, athletic college grants, grants for women, Native Americans, law school grants, nursing college grants, study-abroad grants, and more. The amount of grants and state scholarships available varies by state.

A Few More Ways to Save on Education

Employee/dependent of employee discounts

Do not forget to ask about discounts. For instance, at Mount Carmel College of Nursing in Columbus, Ohio, you can receive a college discount if you are a Mount Carmel employee or the dependent of a Mount Carmel employee. According to the College, "Full-time employees who have completed six months of service are eligible for discounted tuition, as are dependent children (including adopted children and stepchildren) whose parents have completed one year of full-time employment with Mount Carmel." For more information, call 614-234-5800 or 800-556-6942, or visit **www.mccn.edu**.

United States veterans' programs

If you are a United States veteran, you may be eligible to receive educational benefits from a variety of programs:

- IHL (Institutes of Higher Learning)
- NCD (Non-College Degree Programs)
- On-the-Job & Apprenticeship Training
- Flight Training
- Independent Training, Distance Learning, and Internet Training
- Correspondence Training
- National Testing Program
- Licensing and Certification
- Entrepreneurship Training
- Work-Study Program
- Co-op Training
- Accelerated Payment of MGIB-AD

- Tuition Assistance Top-Up
- Tutorial Assistance Program

You can find out more about educational benefits and how to apply at **www.benefits.va.gov/gibill**. You can also call to ask about educational benefits at 800-827-1000.

Office of Special Education and Rehabilitative Services

At the Office of Special Education and Rehabilitative Services (OSERS), certain people with disabilities may apply for various programs designed to help them enter the workforce. According to the OSERS:

> "The Office of Special Education and Rehabilitative Services (OSERS) understands the many challenges still facing individuals with disabilities and their families. Therefore, OSERS is committed to improving results and outcomes for people with disabilities of all ages. OSERS supports programs that serve millions of children, youth, and adults with disabilities."

The office is comprised of the Office of Special Education Programs (OSEP), the National Institute on Disability and Rehabilitation Research (NIDRR), and the Rehabilitation Services Administration (RSA).

According to the U.S. Department of Education, "Through the Office of the Assistant Secretary for Special Education and Rehabilitative Services, OSERS administers programs that support three institutions:

- The American Printing House for the Blind
- The National Technical Institute for the Deaf
- Gallaudet University

For more information, contact OSERS at 202-245-7486, or visit **www.ed.gov**.

The Office of Indian Education Programs

The Office of Indian Education Programs (OIEP) offers educational funds to eligible American Indian/Alaska Native students. According to the OIEP, they include:

- Higher ED Grants to assist those seeking a baccalaureate degree.

- Graduate Fellowship Grants: Designed to assist American Indian college graduates continuing their education at the master's, doctorate, and professional degree level.

- BIA Summer Law Program: American Indian students at the University of New Mexico have the opportunity to participate in a two-month program that prepares prospective lawyers for the rigors of law school.

For more information about these programs and for eligibility requirements (such as some may require you to be an active member of your tribe), visit **www.bie.gov**.

Wrapping It Up

Keep in mind that because these programs come from the government, the rules can change. For example, in recent years, rule changes have made it harder to become eligible for the Pell Grant. Yet, in 2006 more than 300,000 families became eligible for the new Academic Competitiveness Grants and the SMART grants, as these grants are new.

Grants are a great way to help pay for your college education, and you will not have to worry about paying it back. Your student loan payments will not be so hefty, and you will have fewer financial worries while in school as well.

Do not assume that you are not qualified for a grant. Always check with your school's financial aid office to see if you might be eligible. Generally, they will have much of the necessary paperwork to apply for government grants. For private grants, you might check out **www.fastweb.com**.

There are need-based and merit-based grants especially designed for women, minorities, military families, undergraduates, graduates, doctoral students, and more. There is also money out there for veterans and those with a disability. With a lot of research and patience, you can no doubt find grants and other "free money" that you are eligible to receive.

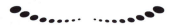

Chapter 5

Learn Now, Pay Later

L et's face it. Most college students end up taking out student loans, unless they are lucky enough to win the lottery, their parents are wealthy enough to cover the cost, or they receive grant money or a scholarship that covers the cost of tuition and room and board.

While student loans are a justifiable loan — since they are helping you attain a degree — they definitely have drawbacks. For one, with a student loan you can have hefty monthly payments, and it could take years to pay it back. Writing out a check every month for $200, $250, $300, $400, or more can be a painful occurrence. You will have other financial obligations every month besides a student loan, such as a mortgage or rent payment, a car payment, utilities, gas, and groceries, which can be difficult to pay on top of your student loan. Unless you are entering into a high-paying career (and very few careers pay well in the early years), you could be struggling and trying to make ends meet for years to come. What you do not want to do if you take out a student loan is take out more money than you really need to get through school. Sure, it may be nice to have the extra money when you are spending it, but you will need to be smart and only use loans for tuition and living if needed. They are money you have to pay back, and there is no getting out of it. If you do not pay your student loans, you will ruin your credit and become ineligible to borrow money for school ever again.

However, loans are a wonderful way to help get through school. Many students could not consider going to college if they were not available. Interest on student loans is about as low as it gets, so you cannot find a cheaper way to borrow money.

Interest rates are an important aspect of borrowing money, as is keeping the principal balance, or the money you borrowed in the first place, down to a minimum.

To show how much interest rates affect payment and interest paid, consider a $20,000 loan that you will pay off in five years. At 18 percent interest, you will pay $507.87 per month with a grand total of $10,472.11 interest paid. Conversely, on that same $20,000 loan with an 8 percent interest rate, your payments will be $405.53, while the interest will cost you an extra $4,331.67. You will save about $6,000 in interest with a $20,000 loan if your interest rate is 8 percent instead of 18 percent. An 18 percent interest rate may seem high, but it is the going rate for many credit cards nowadays.

Rates on student loans, which we will learn more about shortly, are generally in the five to eight percent interest rate range. They are available at a percentage that you will not find easily anywhere else, so if you need to borrow money for college, take out a student loan. Just keep in mind the following:

- You should take only out what you truly need.
- You do not have to borrow the entire amount that is offered to you. You can lower the amount or decline the loan.
- You should figure out what your loan payments will be before you borrow.
- Make sure you estimate what your school costs will be so that you borrow the right amount.
- Read all the paperwork before you sign the loan.
- Compare interest rates on different loans.
- Find out if the loan you are taking out accrues interest while you are in school.
- See if there are any other ways to save. Some lenders cut the interest rate if you sign up for a monthly debit out of your checking or savings account to repay the loan.

To get started on your student loan, you should first complete your FAFSA as described in Chapter 3. Now, let us explore student loans in more detail.

Federal Student Loan Programs

Two main federal programs are the largest source of college loans. One is the Federal Family Education Loan Program (FFELP) and the other one is the William D. Ford Federal Direct Loan Program (FDLP).

The programs offer subsidized loans and unsubsidized loans. Subsidized loans are based on financial need. The interest on subsidized loans will not accrue while you are in school at least half-time and during grace and authorized deferment periods. Unsubsidized loans are not need-based, and you are responsible for all of the interest that accrues on the loan, including while you are in school. You must pay this quarterly, but the amounts are not usually that high.

FFELP loans

According to the U.S. Department of Education website, **www.ed.gov**, loan eligibility and loan type for a Federal Family Education Loan Program (FFELP) are as follows:

- **Stafford:** Individuals who are undergraduate, vocational, or graduate students accepted for enrollment at least half-time in participating schools.

- **Unsubsidized Stafford:** Individuals who are undergraduate, vocational, or graduate students accepted for enrollment at least half-time in participating schools.

- **PLUS:** Individuals who are parents of dependent undergraduate students accepted for enrollment at least half-time in participating schools. As of July 1, 2006, graduate students are also eligible.

- **Consolidation:** Individuals who have outstanding student loans and are in a grace period or repayment status or those who have defaulted but have made satisfactory arrangements to repay their loan(s).

FFELP loans are available through many private banks, credit unions, and education finance companies, so you have a choice of lenders, but you should first ask your school's financial office for their suggestions.

With the Federal Family Education Loan Program (FFELP), rates are very attractive in comparison to many loans. According to the U.S. Department of Education:

- With a Subsidized Stafford loan, the government pays the interest when the student is in school and during periods of grace and deferment. The current interest rate for the 2015-2016 academic year is 4.29 percent.

- With an Unsubsidized Stafford loan, the interest is not paid by the government when the student is in school, nor during periods of grace and deferment. The current interest rate for the 2015-2016 academic year is 4.29 percent.

- With a PLUS loan, parents can borrow to pay the costs of higher education for their dependent undergraduates and graduate students to pay their costs. The current interest rate for the 2015-2016 academic year is 6.84 percent.

- With a Consolidation loan, more than one federal education loan is combined into a single loan. The current interest rate is figured by weighting the average of loans rounded upward to the nearest 1/8 percent. The interest rate was capped at 8.25 percent as of July 1, 2013. This rate is fixed for life.

When shopping around for a FFELP loan, you might want to consider what kind of customer service the lender offers. Do they have an online feature where you can access your loan and pay online? Will they pay any of the up-front fees for borrowers? Do they offer any discounts on the interest rates set by Congress?

FDLP loans

According to the U.S. Department of Education, loan type and eligibility for the William D. Ford Federal Direct Loan Program (FDLP) is as follows:

- **Direct Stafford:** Individuals who are undergraduate, vocational, or graduate students accepted for enrollment at least half-time in participating schools.

- **Direct Unsubsidized Stafford:** Individuals who are undergraduate, vocational, or graduate students accepted for enrollment at least half-time in participating schools.

- **Direct PLUS:** Individuals who are parents of dependent undergraduate students accepted for enrollment at least half-time in participating schools. Beginning July 1, 2006, graduate students are also eligible.

- **Direct Consolidation:** Individuals who have outstanding student loans or those who have defaulted but have made satisfactory arrangements to repay the loan(s) (or who agree to pay under the income contingent repayment plan).

With the William D. Ford Federal Direct Loan Program (FDLP), rates are very attractive in comparison to many loans. According to the U.S. Department of Education:

- With a Direct Stafford loan, the student is not liable for interest when in school and during periods of grace and deferment. The current interest rate for the 2015-2016 academic year is 6.84 percent.

- With a Direct Unsubsidized Stafford loan, the student is liable for interest while in school and during periods of grace and deferment. The current interest rate for the 2015-2016 academic year is 6.84 percent.

- With a Direct PLUS loan, parents can borrow to pay the costs of higher education for their dependent undergraduates and graduate students to pay their costs. The current interest rate for the 2015-2016 academic year is 6.84 percent.

- With a Direct Consolidation loan, more than one federal education loan is combined into a single loan. The current interest rate is figured by weighting the average of loans rounded upward to the nearest 1/8 percent. The interest rate was capped at 8.25 percent as of July 1, 2015.

Before receiving your first Direct Loan, a Master Promissory Note (MPN) must be signed. The MPN outlines the terms and conditions of your loan and is a legally binding agreement to repay your loan. Both the FAFSA and the MPN may be completed online.

To apply for a Direct Loan from the Department of Education, you must first complete your FAFSA as presented in Chapter 3. Your school's financial aid office website has the necessary paperwork, and you can complete the application online at **www.fafsa.ed.gov**.

Unlike other loans, borrowing is directly through the federal government, and loan payments are made to the Department of Education for the life of your loan. The loans are never sold. To save on interest, try to pay off your loans as quickly as possible.

Federal Perkins Loans

The Federal Perkins Loan Program is a loan program that provides low-interest (five percent) loans to "exceptionally" needy students to help pay for the costs of postsecondary education. Nearly 2,000 postsecondary (undergraduate, vocational, and graduate) institutions participate.

Your school determines which students have the greatest need, and then the school combines federal funds with some of the school's own funds for loans to qualifying students. Your school will either pay you directly (a minimum of two payments during the academic year), or apply your loan to your school charges. There are no fees with this loan. The loan limit is $5,500 for undergraduates and $8,000 for graduate students. You have nine months after you graduate for repayment to begin, with the interest rate remaining subsidized.

The requirements for a Federal Perkins loan are:

- You must be enrolled in an eligible school at least half-time in a degree program.
- You must have U.S. citizenship, permanent residency, or eligible noncitizen status.
- You must maintain satisfactory academic progress.
- You must not have any unresolved defaults or overpayments owed on Title IV education loans and grants.
- You must satisfy all Selective Service requirements.

To apply for a Federal Perkins Loan, you must submit the Free Application for Federal Student Aid (FAFSA) at **www.fafsa.ed.gov**.

Federal Stafford Loans

You may have heard of "Stafford Loans" before, yet you may not know what kind of loan it is. In 1988, Congress renamed the Federal Guaranteed Student Loan program the Robert T. Stafford Student Loan program, in honor of Senator Robert Stafford of Vermont for his work in higher education.

Stafford loans refer to the Federal Direct Student Loan Program (FDSLP, also known as Direct Loans), granted directly from the United States Department of Education and the Federal Family Education Loan Program (FFELP), available from a private lender.

Stafford loans are guaranteed by the full faith of the U.S. Government, and they are offered at a lower interest rate than the borrower would otherwise be able to get for a private loan. This means, if the student defaults, the lender is paid by the government. There are strict eligibility requirements and borrowing limits on Stafford loans.

With a Stafford loan, you are receiving either a subsidized (the government pays the interest while you are in school) or unsubsidized (you pay all the interest, but the payments may be deferred until after graduation) loan.

To receive a subsidized Stafford loan, financial need must be demonstrated on your FAFSA. Most subsidized Stafford loans are awarded to students with a family AGI of less than $50,000. All students are generally eligible for the unsubsidized Stafford loan. You can apply for and receive both kinds of loans. Currently, the interest rate is 6.84 percent. It is the rate you should receive from whatever source you get the loan. Check to see if discounts for electronic loan payments or other discounts are available. The loan fee is 4 percent, which is deducted from your disbursement check, and generally the repayment terms are 10 years, but other terms, such as extended payment terms, are available.

How Much Can You Borrow?

According to **https://studentaid.ed.gov**:

> "If you are an undergraduate student, you can borrow $5,500 to
> $12,500 per year from Direct Subsidized and Unsubsidized Loans
> (and graduate students can borrow up to $20,500 yearly in Direct
> Unsubsidized Loans), depending on varying factors and grade
> level. You can borrow up to $5,500 per year in Perkins Loans (and
> for graduate students up to $8,000 yearly), also dependent on
> other factors. Before receiving any loans, you now have to complete
> 'entrance counseling' to make sure you understand your obligations
> in repaying your loans. Your school's financial aid department will
> have more details on how to do this."

When applying for a Stafford loan, you must first complete a Free Application for Federal Student Aid (FAFSA) at **www.fafsa.ed.gov**.

Federal PLUS Loans

The Federal PLUS loan is a parent loan program for parents of undergraduate students that offers an affordable, low-interest solution for parents to help out their dependent children. Independent students are not eligible. Banks and other lending institutions offer these loans.

The loan is not based on household income, assets, or financial need, so most parents are eligible to receive the loan. The loan can be used to cover 100 percent of the cost of education, minus any financial awards already awarded to the student. For instance, if a student received a scholarship for $2,500, that may be deducted from the loan amount parents can receive. The total amount, however, can include tuition as well as books, food, housing, supplies, and other expenses that are intrinsic to attending school.

A few facts about a Federal PLUS loan:

- You must be a U.S. citizen or national, a U.S. permanent resident, or eligible noncitizen.
- A credit check is required.
- Collateral is not required.
- The federal government does not require that you file the Free Application for Federal Student Aid (FAFSA) to qualify for a Parent PLUS loan, but schools do require the FAFSA for Parent PLUS borrowers. Check with your school's financial aid office.
- For loans first disbursed on or after July 1, 2015, the interest is fixed at 8.25 percent.
- The federal government charges a three percent origination fee.
- Payments may be postponed while you child is attending school.
- Interest may be tax deductible. Check with your tax adviser.

Check with your lender about specific details and about applying for the loan.

Parents of graduate students can apply for the Graduate PLUS loan, another low-interest, federally backed student loan guaranteed by the U.S. government. Just like with the Parent PLUS Loan, the loan can be used to pay for the total cost of education, including supplies, books, and even food, minus any financial awards already awarded to the student. Students can postpone repayment of their federal student loans while enrolled at least half-time in a degree or certificate program. Banks and other lending institutions offer these loans.

Repayment terms of PLUS loans are the same as what is outlined in this chapter under Repayment. Options include: Standard repayment, graduated repayment, income-sensitive repayment, and extended repayment.

Service-Cancelable Loans

A service-cancelable loan is just that. You provide a service upon completing school, and your school loan may be cancelled. You must generally work in a "critical need" field for a set number of years. The loans are funded through the government. "Mapping Your Future" has list of opportunities to get your loan cancelled by providing service. The opportunities for these loans range include having 70 percent of your loan cancelled by volunteering in Vista or the Peace Corps or teaching in elementary or secondary schools in a low-income school district and having $5,000 to $17,500 cancelled from your student loan debt. The site below links to an Annual Directory of Designated Low-Income Schools for Teacher Cancellation Benefits. You might also check with your school's financial aid office to see if they have any service-cancelable loan possibilities.

Let us look at a few of the service-cancelable loan possibilities that are listed **www.mappingyourfuture.org**.

Child Care Providers

Certain child care providers who have outstanding federal student loans may be eligible to have their loans

forgiven. In other words, you will not have to repay the amount. To be eligible for loan forgiveness, all of the following criteria must be met:

- You must be a new borrower as of Oct. 1, 1998,
  (i.e., have no outstanding balance on a Federal Family
  Education Loan [FFEL] Program or Federal Direct Program
  loan as of that date).

- You must have obtained an associate's or bachelor's degree
  in early childhood education from an institution of higher

education. If you originally received a degree in another area of study but later obtained a degree in early childhood education, forgiveness will be limited to eligible loans you obtained for a maximum of two of the academic years required to obtain the early childhood education degree.

- You must have worked full-time as a childcare provider in a facility that serves a low-income community for the two consecutive years preceding the year during which you requested loan forgiveness. At least 70 percent of the individuals that facility serves must be from families that earn less than 85 percent of the state median household income.

- You must not have received benefits for the same childcare service under the National and Community Service Act of 1990 (AmeriCorps).

The program is offered on a first-come, first-serve basis, subject to the availability of funds.

Forgiveness Amounts

To be eligible for forgiveness, you must maintain full-time employment for successive, uninterrupted 12-month periods. A proportion of the balance of your FFEL Program or Federal Direct Loans (including interest that accrues) may be forgiven in the following increments:

- 20 percent after completing two consecutive years of qualifying employment
- 20 percent after completing the third consecutive year of qualifying employment
- 30 percent after completing the fourth consecutive year of qualifying employment

- 30 percent after completing the fifth consecutive year of qualifying employment

Public Service Loan Forgiveness Program (PSLF)

The Public Service Loan Forgiveness Program will forgive, or erase the remaining balance on Direct Loans after you have made 120 qualifying monthly payments if you are on the repayment plan and are working full-time for a qualifying employer.

- Agencies that qualify: Any level of Government organizations (federal, state, local, or tribal)
- Non-profit organizations: Must be tax exempt under Section 501 (c) (3)
- Other non-profit organizations that provide qualifying public services

To find out more about all of the requirements, refer to **https://studentaid.ed.gov/sa** and look into your state to see if they have either loan repayment plans or grants for these types of Public Service careers.

Repayment

With many types of loans, you have several repayment options to choose from: standard, extended, graduated, and income contingent. The options can sometimes be changed any time during the life of the loan, so if you start with a standard repayment plan and run into financial hardships along the way, you can find out about an income-contingent repayment plan. You should always find out about payment plans before you agree to any loan. Always find out what the plan options are and whether they can be changed. Check with your lender for specific details before agreeing to accept a loan.

Here is an overview of what the repayment plans typically are:

- **Standard Plan:** A fixed payment every month (generally at least $50), and you have (typically) 10 years to repay your loan.

- **Extended Plan:** A fixed payment every month (generally at least $50), but you have (typically) 12 to 30 years to repay your loan.

- **Graduated Plan:** Payments start out low and increase (generally every two years). You have (typically) up to 30 years to repay the loan. Make sure you know what the maximum amount will increase to.

- **Income-Contingent Repayment Plan:** Each year, your monthly payments will be based off your adjusted gross income (AGI, plus your spouse's income if you are married), family size, and the total amount of your loan.

You can also inquire from your lender about a Student Loan Consolidation.

With loan consolidation, your eligible student loans will be consolidated into a new loan with a single monthly payment and fixed interest rate. Your monthly payments may lower but sometimes with a higher total loan cost with consideration of extra fees. The one problem you may run into though with consolidation is that some repayment loans (such as teaching) do not want the amount that may be paid back consolidated into other loans. Your lender should be able to help you with this.

If you run into financial hardship, return to school at least part-time, are on active duty during war, national emergency, or military operation, or encounter other serious hardships, you may request a period of deferment so you can temporarily postpone payment of your loan. Keep in mind that you must apply and be approved for a deferment. Different loans have different deferment requirements. Always contact your lender directly about a deferment.

You can also request what is called "forbearance." You can reduce your monthly loan payment should you be approved for one. The length of the loan is extended for forbearances. Often, the amount of time it takes to repay your loan is extended.

If you run into any trouble making payments on your loan, try to work something out with the lender. Generally, you can reach a doable agreement so that your loan does not default and ruin your credit. Work something out with them as soon as you can. It is better not to wait until you miss a payment to make the call. Lenders are more apt to work with you if you call early and do not have a habit of being late with your payments.

There are certain circumstances allowing your student loan to be discharged, including the event of your death, if you become totally and permanently disabled after the loan is disbursed, if the school you were attending closed(in certain bankruptcy cases), or if your loan was falsely certified by an eligible school (i.e. signing your name without permission). You can find out more about loan discharges at the U.S. Department of Education website, **www.ed.gov**.

Private Loans

After you have exhausted all of your federal borrowing options, you may find you still need more funds. That is why some are turning to private loans to fill the gaps. Private loans are ones that are procured from a bank, a lending institution, or even a credit card. Interest rates on private school loans are often credit-based, meaning the better the credit, the lower the interest. Before you (or your parents) consider taking out a private loan, plenty of research needs to be done. Here are some of the questions you should find out the answer to before you agree to the loan:

- What is the interest rate?
- Is the interest rate fixed or variable?
- What are the fees?
- What are the repayment options?
- What are the borrower benefits, such as discounts, customer service, and online servicing?
- Is there a prepayment penalty?
- Will this count as income when I do my tax return? (If this is the case, you need to find another lender.)

You need to read all of the loan documents that you are agreeing to. Do not sign anything unless you fully understand what you are signing. There may be hidden fees and clauses that you do not notice at first. All lenders have different requirements.

Ask your school's financial aid department if they have a list of private loan lenders or your bank or your parents' bank if they have private school loans available.

One more source to try for a private loan is through your family. You might ask a relative or your parents if you can borrow money from them. You could work out a loan agreement that is similar to what you may have gotten from a government loan, with low interest and payments over an extended time. Or you could offer to make them a deal they cannot turn down, such as an offer to pay them higher rates than they may have gotten elsewhere. Otherwise, you could ask your relatives or parents if they could consider it as an advanced inheritance. You could work out an arrangement that they pay the school directly and even fill out a loan agreement with the terms spelled out.

If it is a gift, there is good news. A tax-free gift of up to $10,000 per year may be given, as it is called an "annual exclusion." Always check with your financial adviser before making assumptions about gifting and tax savings.

Bank Loans

You have several options when getting a private loan for undergraduate, graduate, law, dental, or medical school studies. Some of the loans can be for as little as $1,000, while others can go up to more than $200,000. Many private bank loans offer repayment options. As with other loans, you should shop around and find one that best suits your needs.

Some banks vary on loans depending on what state they are in. As in grants, terms, amount and types of loans and condition change depending on the availability of funds. Here are just a couple examples of bank loans:

Wells Fargo offers education loans that will fund up to the cost of your education. Students make no payments while in school. Go to **www.wellsfargo.com** for more information.

SunTrust Bank offers an Academic Answer® loan for undergraduate and graduate studies. $65,000 or your school's cost of attendance, whichever is less, with total loan limit of $150,000. You can find out more at **www.suntrusteducation.com**.

Many banks offer their own student loan programs. It is best to start with your own bank to see what they might offer for student loans. Loan types and terms vary depending on the institution. Make sure you read and understand all of your loan documents before agreeing to a loan. Always inquire about the following:

- Find out what the fees are.
- Understand what the repayment terms are.
- Know what the interest rate is.
- Find out when your payments begin.
- Know what your payments will be.
- Learn where the loan funds go — directly to you? Or to the school?

Home Equity Alternatives

If you have home equity, or your parents do, you can consider home equity as a source for funding college.

So what is home equity? Home equity is the portion of your home's value that you own, versus what the lender owns. For instance, if your home's fair market value is $200,000 and your outstanding loan on your home totals $130,000, that would mean you have $70,000 in home equity.

Home equity is a valuable asset that you can tap into for funds, and you do not have to sell your home in order to get the money. Your home is your collateral for the loan. However, if you default on a home equity loan, your lender could foreclose on it. Yes, you could lose the home if you do not make your loan payments.

Home equity loans generally have some fees. There are fees for closing costs, for setting up the loan, applying for the loan, recording the loan, and performing a property survey and title search, as well as others. Often the repayment terms are anywhere from five to 20 years, depending on the amount you borrowed. If you sell your home, the loan must be paid back in full.

There are two basic types of home equity loans:

- **Term Equity Loan:** A lump sum, fixed-interest-rate loan with the same payments every month.

- **Home Equity Line of Credit:** You borrow what you need, and generally pay a variable interest rate.

When your payment time expires, you must pay off the balance, or apply to extend or renew the loan or line of credit. Fees vary depending on the lender.

You can receive a home equity loan or line of credit from a variety of lenders and banks. They do not have to be the originator of any of your previous loans. For instance, you can have a first home loan with ABC Lender and get a home equity loan from XYZ Bank.

While your parents can borrow money against their home, they may want to consider downsizing their home instead. If the market is right and they are looking for a smaller residence anyway, maybe now is the time to sell and use some of the funds to help pay for your college education. Besides freeing up some cash, there are capital gains to consider. Capital gains on personal real estate are tax free up to $500,000 for couples and $250,000 for singles with certain restrictions, like living on the property for a certain number of years. Ask your tax adviser for details. That means you can make that much on a real estate sale without paying hefty capital gains taxes. Not only that, moving to a smaller residence can help save on your overall expenses, such as maintenance, insurance, utilities, and taxes. But do not just take for granted that your parents will do this just to help pay for your college education, as it is quite a lot to ask of them. This is only in the case that they were thinking of downsizing in the first place.

Retirement Fund Borrowing

One of the last places you or your parents should look for college funding is in your retirement plan. Before tapping into a retirement fund, it is a good idea to have exhausted all of your other resources. You should have applied for every possible grant and scholarship, taken advantage of student loans and private loans, and checked into home equity before dipping into a 401(k).

If you must borrow from your or your parents' 401(k) plan, keep in mind that certain tax rules limit the amount you can use as a loan. Tax advantages are not available like with certain other loans, including a home equity loan where you can deduct the interest. With retirement fund borrowing, you can typically borrow up to 50 percent of your vested account balance or $50,000 — whichever is less. Although you do not have to qualify for the loan, as it is money you are borrowing from yourself, remember when the money is taken out it is no longer earning money for your or your parents' retirement. Do not assume that this is something that is doable, let alone possible, for your parents to do.

Before you take any money out of a 401(k) plan, you should always:

- Check the interest rate on the loan against your 401(k).
- Find out about an early withdrawal penalty if you do not pay the loan back. It may be as large as 10 percent.

- Do not assume your 401(k) plan allows for loans, though most do.
- Find out what the repayment terms are.

It is best to speak with a tax adviser first. Taking money out of your retirement account can end up costing you more than you anticipated if you do not know the guidelines for how much money you can borrow against your 401(k) for your particular situation.

Keep in mind that you should never borrow any money that is going to put your own retirement, or your parents' retirement, in jeopardy. While they may want to pitch in to help their child, or you may feel that your parents "owe" you, the later years of life need to be planned as well. Heading into retirement years with nothing in the bank is a bad financial move. While your parents may be able to help you out with college, you need to keep their own financial situation in mind and try to exhaust other resources first.

Wrapping It Up

Your best bet for finding a good rate on a student loan is through one of the several government student loan programs. Certain careers and schools offer opportunities for service-cancelable loans. That means that under certain circumstances, like teaching in a low-income area for a specified amount of years, you will not have to pay the loan, or at least part of the loan, back. Home equity loans are a possible loan source if you or your parents have equity in a home. Retirement borrowing against your 401(k) is possible, but check with your tax adviser before you consider taking out any money from your retirement savings. Borrowing from your nest egg should usually be the last thing you consider. To make extra income you can work either during the school year or during the summer months while you may not be in school. Remember, the less money that you have to borrow, the better.

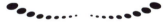

Chapter 6

Work It Out!

ven with grants, scholarships, and loans, sometimes it is a good idea to supplement your college years with extra work. Working off some of your college costs can reduce your need for more loans. Remember, loans are money that you have to start paying back generally six months after graduation. Besides lowering your borrowed money amount, work opportunities (if in your major area) give you helpful training so that when you graduate you will have some experience in your field. Once you are done with school and looking for a job, having that extra edge of experience is helpful in landing a better job that much sooner. In addition, working while in school can provide you with a contact base that will be helpful for you to tap into when you are looking for a career. For instance, you may have a summer job and your manager suddenly receives a higher position at a better company — a company that you always wanted to work for. Well,

now you personally know someone who works there, and they might be able to help you get in the door.

Let us look at some of the opportunities you can exploit to work your way through college.

CASE STUDY: SHAUN FAWCETT, M.b.a. Of Final Draft Publications

Here are 10 tips for writing a winning résumé.

1.   Keep It Focused and Businesslike

A résumé should be specific and all business. Remember, you are asking an employer to invest significant time and money by choosing you over other similarly qualified people.

2.   More Than Two Pages Is Too Much

For students, recent graduates, or people with just a few years of experience, try to keep your résumé to one page, two as an absolute maximum.

3.   Get the Words and Punctuation Right

Make sure the grammar, spelling, and punctuation in your résumé are perfect. Keep the language clear and simple. If you draft it yourself, have someone with excellent writing skills do an editorial review and a careful proofread. Refer to an English language "style guide" to double-check.

4.   Read Between the Lines

Customize the résumé to match the stated requirements of the job that you are applying for, without being misleading. Review and analyze the job ad carefully. Itemize the key qualifications, skills, and abilities the employer is seeking. When possible, study the company's annual report and website, and weave the themes and terms found there into your résumé and cover letter.

5.   Make Sure It Looks Good

Use a crisp, clean, simple presentation format for a professional-looking résumé. Just a bit of simple line work and/or shading will do the trick. If you need help, ask your friends seek professional advice.

6.   Show What You Can Do Today

Focus first on your recent experience that is most relevant to the position at hand. Less relevant and/or dated experience should be either eliminated or summarized in brief point form near the end of your résumé.

7.   Be a Straight Shooter

Be completely honest. When people lie or "creatively exaggerate" on their résumé, they are almost invariably exposed, sooner or later. Think about it — who really wants to get a job based on a lie(s) and then have to live in fear of eventually being found out?

8.   Follow the Instructions

Submit your résumé in exactly the form that the prospective employer requests. If they say email, fax, or snail mail, send it that way. If using snail mail, use the complete address that they specify so it arrives in the right location.

9.   Do Not Get Lost in the Mail

Be careful to respect certain conventions that the prospective employer may require in your résumé. For example, make sure that the cover letter mentions the exact name of the specific position you are applying for and the competition number, if applicable.

---

10. Do Not Repeat Yourself

In the cover letter, do not repeat what is already detailed in the body of the résumé. Introduce yourself first, then briefly summarize why you believe that you have the qualifications and experience to fulfill the duties of the position. Express enthusiasm. Close by stating how you are looking forward to hearing more from them soon and that you will follow up if necessary.

And last of all, remember that most people do not like to read, so be brief (do not bore them), but catch their attention with the most important or valuable things about yourself first.

Work and Service Opportunities

If you are looking to land work during college, you might want to check the college bulletin to see if any opportunities are posted. Another good source is to check in the local papers under the want ads. Temporary work and even long-term opportunities can be found through temporary agencies like Kelly Services (**www.kellyservices.us**) and Manpower, Inc., (**www.us.manpower.com**). Although temp agencies may specialize in temporary work, they offer permanent jobs as well. Some of the temp agencies allow you to apply for work online, although an initial interview may be required. Just remember that many of these agencies charge you a fee to find you a job that you might be able to get for yourself first, so resort to these as a last choice. Many businesses advertise for help with "Help Wanted" signs in their windows, while other, larger companies have ongoing needs for new employees year-round. Many times if you have a part-time job in in your hometown and that business is also in your college town, they will transfer you when you start college, but you need to ask and not just assume that they will do that. Some jobs will be better preparations for after graduation, so you might want to consider trying to find any work you can in your field. For instance, accounting students may look for seasonal tax work at H&R Block, while law students may want to seek work in a law library. A foot in the door can really lead to that door opening up to future opportunities for you.

The federal government also offers a Federal Work-Study (FWS) program, a need-based employment program for full-time undergraduate, graduate, and professional students. According to the U.S. Department of Education, "The FWS Program provides funds that are earned through part-time employment to assist students in financing the costs of post-secondary education." This federally funded program is offered at approximately 3,400 participating post-secondary institutions. Hourly wages must not be less than the federal minimum wage (and many times are above that). You can also possibly find one that is in your department of your major, which can be another benefit. Jobs are often posted at the school's campus or on the school's website. You can find out more about the Federal Work-Study program at **www.ed.gov**. Ask your financial aid office for more details and Federal Work-Study possibilities at your school.

Service opportunities are also something to consider. They play a role in providing service to the community, with work opportunities through agencies such as the United Way, the American Red Cross, and Habitat for Humanity. Other service opportunities can be found in local theaters, groups, or even churches. Service opportunities can even be geared toward your major. For instance, a theater major may find that working for a local theater makes sense, while nursing students may benefit from working with the Red Cross. Some of the service opportunities are unpaid positions, while others give small stipends. You might ask your college if academic credit can be earned with a service opportunity. Either way, service opportunities provide great benefits to the community and may also give you experience in your career field.

Something to consider before figuring out what job suits you during college is to conduct an information interview. That is where you meet with people who are already working in your chosen career and ask questions about particular occupations or companies. This gives you a personal perspective on what the job would entail, plus it never hurts to make a career contact. A few questions to ask are what do you love about your job, what do you dislike about it? Describe the best day ever, and describe the worse day as well. What is a typical day, a hectic day, a slow day? Were there any particular college classes that might help with the degree?

You might want to try job shadowing. Job shadowing is where you visit a business and observe one or more positions at work, whether for an hour or a day. This again gives you the benefit of understanding a position more, while offering you an opportunity to make another contact.

Getting early experience in your career helps you out in many ways, such as:

- **Earning money:** You are earning some money even with part-time jobs.
- Résumé building: You are gaining some work experience, which is good for your résumé.
- **Getting your feet wet:** You may be learning about your field before you finish school.
- **Career choice:** You may find that there are other career choices in your field and find one that might suit you even better than the one you had planned.
- **Networking:** You may be making contacts that will help later on in your job search.
- **Learning skills:** You are learning new skills such as knowing how to work as a team and learning how to do a specific task.

When looking for a job, and even after you have found one, remember to:

- Keep your résumé up-to-date.
- Start to build a network. Get names and numbers of those whom you might contact later.
- Get your letters of recommendation. It is easier to get them now, rather than backtrack.
- If applicable, start to build your portfolio. Make sure you get copies of what you have worked on.

To find a job, try the following:

- Check the want ads.
- Ask at your school's career center.
- Look at bulletin boards.
- Go to job fairs.
- Ask friends, family, and fellow students if they have heard of anything available.
- Make cold calls. Either call businesses or stop in and fill out an application.
- Sign up at temp agencies. Sometimes temp jobs turn into longer jobs.
- Register with an agency in person and/or online.

Cooperative Education

Cooperative education combines secondary education with work experience that is practical for the focus of your studies. You receive academic credit and pay that varies according to your major, the employer, the job's location, the position, and your qualifications for the job. Often the programs are designed to have you alternate semesters of academic study with semesters of full-time employment in positions related to your academic or career interests, although there are other situations. Some colleges offer programs with cooperative education, and others do not, while some focus entirely on cooperative education. For instance, NC State University, the largest university in North Carolina, has 10 colleges with most major academic disciplines, as well as graduate school with programs in over 100 areas.

According to NC State University, "We integrate the opportunities our world-class research programs offer students into our degree tracks and emphasize innovation and on-the-job experience. Instruction at NC State begins in the classroom, but it almost always leads into laboratories — where students work side-by-side with leading researchers in their fields — or to stages, galleries, and off-campus job internships and co-ops that expose students to real-world challenges and experiences. By the time most NC State students graduate, they have not only mastered their area of expertise, they have gained valuable job experience (and often job offers) and discovered the potential for inquiry and creativity within themselves." For more information, contact www.ncsu.edu.

NC State's program is a great way to get started in your career while gaining school credit along the way.

Another school whose focus is cooperative education is the University of North Texas, which offers undergraduate and graduate degrees in all kinds of subjects, including aerospace studies, business, and political science.

According to the university, "Most programs offer hands-on experience in your field before graduation. Internships provide invaluable training and a head start on your career. UNT's nationally accredited Cooperative Education program provides students with paid, supervised positions related to their field of study, often for several semesters. Some students even receive academic credit for their work and/or permanent job offers after graduation." For more information, visit www.unt.edu.

Some of the benefits with receiving a cooperative education are:

- Practical experience in your field of study.
- Your education is applied to real-life work situations.
- You make useful contacts.
- You learn real-life working skills.
- You earn money.

A great source of information about cooperative education is with the National Commission for Cooperative Education. According to the Commission, "The National Commission for Cooperative Education (NCCE) is dedicated to advancing cooperative education throughout the United States. Since 1962, the Commission and its college and business partners have supported the development of quality work-integrated learning programs through: National Advocacy, Executive Outreach, Public Awareness, Students & Parent Response Center, and Research & Education."

The Commission developed a co-op model to define what cooperative education should consist of. The characteristics for this model, as detailed on their website, are:

- Formal recognition by the school as an educational strategy integrating classroom learning and progressive work experiences, with a constructive academic relationship between teaching faculty and co-op faculty or administrators.

- Structure for multiple work experiences in formalized sequence with study leading to degree completion of an academic program.

- Work experiences that include an appropriate learning environment and productive work. Work experiences related to career or academic goals. Formal recognition of the co-op experience on student records (e.g. grade, credit hours, part of degree requirement, notation on transcript, etc.). Pre-employment preparation for students, as well as ongoing advising.

- Agreement among the school, employer, and the student on:

  » Job description and new learning opportunities.

  » Specified minimum work periods (equivalent in length to an academic term (quarter, semester, or trimester). In alternating programs, students work approximately 40 hours per week, full-time during the term. In parallel programs, students work approximately 20 hours per week, part-time during the term.

  » Work monitored by the school and supervised by employers.

  » Official school enrollment during employment.

  » Recognition as a co-op employee by the employer.

  » Evaluations by the student, the school, and the employer, with guided reflection by the student.

  » Remuneration for the work performed.

- Provision for employer and school evaluation of quality and relevance of the work experience and curriculum designed to maximize outcomes for students, employers, and the school.

You can find out more about the Commission at **www.co-op.edu**.

Internships

One way to gain work experience in your field of study and perhaps receive academic credit for the hours spent working is with internships. Internships are approved and monitored work experience related to your field of study that meet learning goals. Some internships can help you receive academic credit. To receive credit for your internship, you generally have to get the internship approved beforehand by your school. Some schools have an office that is in charge of helping to find internships for students and many organizations at your school, if connected to your major, have them as well. However, even if you school does not offer academic credit for internships or assist you with finding an internship, they may be worth pursuing on your own. Some of the benefits of internships include:

- You will gain a deeper understanding about a career.
- You will have work experience in your field once you graduate.
- You will be able to find out if you are pursuing the right career.
- You will learn valuable skills.
- You will make connections and start to network.
- If you are planning to go to graduate school, you have an extra edge on your application.
- Many internships not only pay, but some pay rather well.

Before you find out how to get an internship, you might first try to decide what kind interests you and what you hope to gain from it. Figure out what kind of company you would like to work for. Is it a large company or a small one? Ask yourself if you will only take a paid internship or if you are willing to work in an unpaid position. Also think about how long of an internship you are interested in.

Once you have pondered what you want from an internship, you have to find one. You might first ask your school adviser or department head if they know where to look. There may be plenty of resources at your school to help you find an internship, such as a bulletin board with a listing, their website, or an internship adviser on staff. You could always try to tap your family and friends for possibilities as well. Perhaps your uncle works for a company you are interested in interning at. Why not give him a call? There are also websites like Monster (**www.monstertrak.monster.com**) or VAULT (**www.vault. com**) with internship listings. You can always research the company you are interested in and see if they have something posted on their website about internships and who to contact. You might also try local career fairs, as some companies have information about internships available at fairs and other recruitment events.

Always make sure to find out if you can get college credit for your internship. Your school adviser should know if that is possible.

College Work Programs

If you are interested in working while in school, you can apply for a variety of programs at your school that are designed to enhance your education.

The Federal Work-Study Program (FWS) was formerly known as the College Work-Study Program. According to the U.S. Department of Education:

> "The FWS Program provides funds that are earned through part-time employment to assist students in financing the costs of postsecondary education. Students can receive FWS funds at approximately 3,400 participating postsecondary institutions. Institutional financial aid administrators at participating institutions have substantial flexibility in determining the amount of FWS awards to provide to students who are enrolled or accepted

for enrollment. Hourly wages must not be less than the federal minimum wage."

The Federal Work-Study Program (FWS) helps you contribute to your education by enhancing already acquired skills and learning new skills while employed either on-campus or in a community service role.

Generally, the process to apply for a work-study program is to complete the FAFSA, as described in Chapter 3, and then complete an application at your school should they offer this program. You must meet the financial requirements according to FAFSA and maintain academic success, as defined by your school, in order to participate in this program while you attend school. Another advantage of the Work-Study Program is that it often pays more than minimum-wage jobs.

In addition to the Federal Work-Study Program (FWS), certain schools offer their own program designed for those that are not eligible for the FWS. Depending on the school, opportunities may be posted for students to apply for, or students may propose their own jobs at the school and see if they can receive approval for a position. Some schools have work-study coordinators in charge of work-study programs, while others may have less structure to how work-study programs are procured. Some may even require that you maintain a certain GPA. Below are a few work-study scenarios.

At Sterling College in Vermont, **www.sterlingcollege.edu**, the College Work Program requires that you work on campus while attending school:

"In addition to fulfilling academic responsibilities, students function as integral members of the work force of the college. They work at least 80 hours per semester. In exchange for work, students are eligible to earn a minimum $1,650 in tuition and book credit per semester. Many students earn more than that amount by doing additional work. For example, they may have other work-study positions, summer internships, or even residence hall supervision."

Loyola University New Orleans offers a College Work Study (CWS) that "is a federal financial aid work program funded by Loyola University and the United States Department of Education." You can find paid work-study opportunities at **http://studentaffairs.loyno.edu/residential-life/work-study-program**. The jobs pay from $8.25 to $9.00 per hour, and most jobs average about 10 hours per week. Students must first complete their FAFSA, while a College Work Study Coordinator assists with helping you participate in the program.

Alderson-Broaddus College offers the Job Book, located online, that has a listing of all possible job openings, as well as an explanation of how to apply for them. You may earn up to $1,500 a year ($750 per semester) for the federal/college work program. You must complete your FAFSA first, and you are then awarded a work program by the financial aid office. You can find out more at **www.ab.edu**.

At Columbia College in Chicago, Illinois, you can take advantage of the federal work-study program. According to the college (and others as well):

- The Student Financial Services (SFS) Office awards FWS to eligible students each year who demonstrate financial need on the Free Application for Federal Student Aid (FAFSA).

- FWS will appear on the Financial Aid Award Letter from SFS. Students may not earn more than the FWS award amount that appears on the award letter. The funds are not applied to the student's account. The majority of work-study jobs are on-campus. Some students may work for non-profit organizations in the FWS Community Service Program.

- FWS is not a grant. Students must get a job to earn the award. The Student Employment Office will assist students in finding a work-study job. All students must have the proper identification documents to complete a job application in the Student Employment Office.

Ask your academic adviser if there are work-study opportunities at your school, as it is great way to earn money while you learn and many positions are right on campus.

AmeriCorps/National Service

Take advantage of an opportunity to work for AmeriCorps and you could earn a Segal AmeriCorps Education Award equivalent to the maximum value of the Pell Grant ($5,775 as of Oct. 2015-which can change year to year) to pay for college, graduate school, or to pay back qualified student loans. While you work for AmeriCorps you are helping those across the country in community service positions. According to AmeriCorps, the positions range from the chance to:

- Tutor and mentor disadvantaged youth
- Fight illiteracy
- Improve health services
- Build affordable housing
- Teach computer skills
- Clean parks and streams
- Manage or operate after-school programs
- Help communities respond to disasters
- Build organizational capacity

You are paid a "modest living allowance during service, and once you complete your service you can apply for the Segal AmeriCorps Education Award."

There are several programs that you can apply for, including the AmeriCorps State and National that offers national projects in every state, U.S. territory, and on tribal reservations. There is also AmeriCorps VISTA, a national service program designed specifically to fight poverty. The AmeriCorps NCCC (National Civilian Community Corps) is a residential program for men and women age 18 to 24. According the AmeriCorps: "In partnership with nonprofit organizations, state and local agencies, and faith-based and other community organizations, members complete service projects throughout the region they are assigned."

You can apply for AmeriCorps and find out more about the Segal AmeriCorps Education Award and other Corps as well at **www.national service.gov/programs/americorps**.

In addition to helping communities, you are adding great experience for your résumé, plus getting a chance to receive a scholarship for your education.

Reserves/National Guard/R.O.T.C

If you have thought about joining the National Guard or the Reserves, you may be pleased to hear about their program College First, which is designed to allow you to attend undergraduate or graduate school full-time, all while earning over $2,000 per month, with a guarantee of no deployment during your first two years of Guard service. According to the National Guard, "The program also includes many financial benefits that could potentially pay for your entire education."

The National Guard states that you are eligible if:

- You have no experience in the military.
- You are a high school graduate or graduating senior.
- You score 50 or higher on the Armed Services Vocational Aptitude Battery (ASVAB).
- You agree to complete Advanced Individual Training (AIT) immediately following Basic Training.
- You are accepted by a U.S. Department of Education-accredited college or university within 90 days of completing AIT.
- You remain a student in good standing for the duration of your non-deployment period.
- You meet all other National Guard enlistment standards.

What do you get?

- Up to two years of non-deployment following completion of Initial Active Duty Training (IADT)

- An enlistment bonus of up to $20,000.

- The Montgomery G.I. Bill — Selected Reserve (MGIB-SR), basic educational assistance of $317 per month

- The MGIB-SR Kicker — additional educational assistance of $350 per month (available to those enlisting in a critical MOS and assigned to a qualified unit)

- 100 percent Federal tuition assistance, up to $4,500 per year

- Up to 100 percent state tuition assistance; up to $4,300 per year, amount varies by state.

- Recruiting Assistant Pay (Voluntary): This is a 100 percent optional, performance-based program open to Guard members to assist in helping recruit for your unit. Recruiting Assistants (RAs) can earn additional income assisting Guard recruiting efforts, by identifying well-qualified men and women for service in the ARNG. RAs earn $2,000 for each new recruit who enlists and reports to Basic Training or for each prior service member who affiliates with a unit for four months. Monthly dollar amount is based on one referral enlisting each quarter.

The Army National Guard funds up to 100 percent of tuition costs and fees, with amounts varying state-to-state and year-to-year.

Contact your local recruiter for details about College First in your state. Or visit **www.nationalguard.com** to find out more about the Reserves or the National Guard and what college benefits are available to you.

ROTC

There are also ROTC scholarships available at specific colleges. These vary in amounts, some paying stipends along with up to 100 percent tuition. Of course, there are requirements and stipulations. Your best course of action would be to contact the colleges and recruiters.

Wrapping It Up

A great way to lower your college costs is by working off some of the costs. There are plenty of ways you can do so, including work-study opportunities, internships, and cooperative education. If you are inclined to join the National Guard, Reserves, or a college ROTC you might find that they offer several ways to help you pay for college. Paying for college along the way leads to lower student loans and bills that you will be responsible for upon graduation. Plus, working your way through college helps pay your personal expenses while you attend school.

No matter what job you are working in or what program you are working for, keep in mind the following tips while you work.

- Be on time for work.
- Do not leave early or take long lunches, unless approved by your supervisor.
- Do not bad-mouth others that you work with. The grapevine leaves a nasty trail.
- Accept constructive criticism rather than getting angry about it.
- Ask for feedback, especially if you do not receive a formal review.
- Be a team player.
- Always put your best foot forward.

Chapter 7

The Scholarship Jungle

A scholarship is an award of access to an institution or a financial aid award for an individual student scholar for the purpose of furthering their education. Scholarships are awarded based on a variety of criteria that usually reflect the values and purposes of the donor or founder of the award."

Scholarships are another form of "free money" for school. That is why it is in your best interest to explore what is available and what you might be eligible to receive. Like grants, though, it takes time and effort to find and apply for scholarships.

As with grants, there are different types of scholarships, such as:

- **Merit-based:** Determined by your ability in sports, academics, or other areas

- **Need-based:** Determined by you and your family's financial situation
- **Ethnicity-based:** Determined by your race, religion, or national origin
- **Institutional-based:** Awarded by some colleges or universities
- **Community Service-based:** Determined by the hours and the dedication to the service you gave
- **Essay-based:** Determined by the creativity of an essay required
- **Other:** Scholarships are awarded for a number of reasons, sometimes including all of the above

When applying for a scholarship, you should remember that:

- You should apply as early as you can — high school is a good time to start, and your senior year is most likely the best year of your life to apply as not only are there more local scholarships offered than any other time, but your competition is not as fierce as other years.

- The more scholarships that you apply for, the more likely you are to receive one or more.

- Do not assume that because a scholarship is small that it does not count. It all adds up. Even one for only $100 might still pay for a book or two.

- Pay attention to details when filling out all of your forms. Make sure everything is right in terms of content and that it has no grammatical errors. You do not want to miss a scholarship because you forgot to include something or used the wrong color ink.

- Everyone can find some kind of scholarship they are qualified to receive.

- Keep looking even after you think you have exhausted your possibilities.

- Do not stop at one. You may be eligible to receive more. Apply, Apply, Apply!

During this chapter, you will learn the many ways you can find scholarships, but before we do, let us explore some of the areas where you can find out about college funds from sources you may not have considered before.

- Try networking for scholarships. Ask your college friends, your instructors, your relatives, your neighbors, or anyone else who has gone to college or knows someone in college. They may know about a scholarship that you may not have heard of.

- Do not forget about asking at your school's financial aid office. While many scholarships are awarded from private sources, your school may be familiar with some of them. Go to the department head of your major. Sometimes they know of specific ones dealing with that major. Look for any alumni clubs of colleges in your area as well.

- Read your local papers, and listen for ads on local radio and television stations. You would be surprised how often scholarship opportunities are written about or advertised by these methods.

- Review bulletin boards and newsletters. You may spot a scholarship opportunity on your school's bulletin board or at a local business. College newsletters are also good sources for finding scholarships.

- Check directly with non-profit organizations, such as the Red Cross and the YMCA, as well as churches, synagogues, and houses of worship.

- Check with your labor union if either of your parents work for one. They may have scholarship money.

- Ask at your local Chamber of Commerce. They may be aware of different scholarships offered in your community.

- Check with your parents' work. If no one knows of one or they are not sure, and it is a large company, then go to the top.

- Check with any organizations that your parents belong to. Many of them have scholarships for members' children.

- Check directly with your college. Certain colleges have scholarships funds for students who excel but have limited funds.

- If you are still in high school, check with the senior guidance counselor, as many scholarships are sent to their attention.

Defining Yourself

Defining yourself is learning how to display yourself in the best possible way to receive the most scholarship money that you can. You should begin this process as early as possible.

There are some things that you should keep in mind for college even while you are still in high school. These will better prepare you to receive scholarship funds and other opportunities. They include such things as:

- Go to the best high school that you can. If you go to a public school, check the background of the school you are attending to find out its success rate. In some states, such as Florida, the schools are actually graded on test scores and other factors. The best schools receive an A+. If you are looking at private schools, find out the ratio of what kids got into better colleges. Also, make sure that they offer higher-level classes.

- Even if you cannot choose your school, you generally have a say about what classes you can take. Speak to your guidance counselor as early as you can and see what classes would best help prepare you for your college studies. For instance, if you are headed to a degree in engineering, it makes sense to study higher-level math.

- At some schools you can receive college credit for high school classes by taking Advanced Placement (AP) courses. Again, your guidance counselor should be able to help.

- You will want to start exploring colleges as early as possible, just to get an idea of what the college(s) you are interested in expect(s) from new students, as well as to get a feel for that particular school.

- Think about involving yourself with community services and extracurricular activities. Many schools are looking for well-rounded individuals, and all of this helps to get you into the school you want. Be consistent in this as well. Do not join 10 different clubs for one or two years each. You are better off staying with two or three for three or four years while you are in school as it shows commitment on your part.

- Start networking now. You may be surprised how early networking leads to later jobs and other opportunities.

- If you have performed community services or have an excellent status while working part-time in school, it never hurts to start collecting letters of recommendation. That way, the information will be fresh in the minds of those who can write letters for you, and it saves you from backtracking later on.

- If you plan on working during high school, see if you can work in your field or something related. For instance, if you are studying science, perhaps you can get a part-time job in a lab, hospital, or at a veterinarian's office.

Once you are ready to begin college, you will have a long list of things to do in order to help define yourself and figure out the scholarships that you might be entitled to receive. In Chapter 8, we will cover more specifics on the scholarship process, such as writing the essay and filling out your application. However, before that we will explore how to express who you are and how you can position yourself to apply for scholarships effectively.

Some of the items that you will be collecting and working on to help describe or sell yourself for a scholarship are listed below. Again, we will cover these in detail in Chapter 8:

- **Letters of recommendation:** Either from a teacher, an alumnus, an employer, a leader in your church, a prominent member or your community, a coach, or anyone else that can point out your strengths. You also will most likely need one from someone in administration (required by many scholarships). This would include your principal, assistant principal, or guidance counselor. Be sure to give them a résumé of all of your accomplishments, including academic awards, extracurricular activities (sports, clubs, any organization that you belong to), and community service. Most of these people do not know all that you do, and the résumé will only help them write a better letter.

- **An essay:** The college essay you write serves the purpose of convincing admission officers that you should be admitted into their school because of what you have to offer in terms of academic achievements, community service, athletic abilities, and so on. But the most common scholarship essay is the one asking about your goals, college and career.

- **Personal statement:** The above could also be a statement along with another essay topic. Often you are asked to write a just personal statement that highlights your goals and why you are the best applicant for the scholarship.

When working on defining yourself and figuring out what kinds of scholarships that you might be eligible for, you might want to start with a list of achievements that covers the following:

- **School achievements:** What are school achievements that you can say you have accomplished? Were you in sports? Were you on the debate team? Did you volunteer? What were your grades? Did you work part-time?

- **School contacts:** Who do you know from your school years that could possibly write you a letter of recommendation?

Your teacher? Your boss? Your coach? A community leader? A member of your church, synagogue, or place of worship? Remember that they cannot be related to you, and make sure that they like you as well.

- **School degrees/certificates:** Do you have a high school diploma, a two-year degree, a bachelor's degree, or vocational training? Or what degree are you planning to obtain?

- **Contacts:** Who do you know that can help you get into a school? Do you know anyone that went to a school that you are interested in? Can they help with a scholarship letter of recommendation as well? Do you know key members of the community? Do you know anyone that holds a political office?

- **Your interests:** What are you interested in? Do you have favorite pastimes? Hobbies? Are you an expert on a subject matter?

- **Memberships:** Are you a member of a club or a community organization?

- **Your strengths:** What are you good at? What would others say that you are good at? Are you a good communicator? Do you have leadership skills?

- **Your focus on studies:** What do you plan on majoring in? What do you plan on minoring in? Are you heading for a bachelor degree, a master's degree, or a Ph.D.?

- **Your focus with a career:** What do you see yourself doing for a living? Do you have a five-year goal with your career? A 10-year goal? For instance, if you are headed for law school, do you want to work for a firm for a few years and then start your own firm?

- **Your paperwork:** Do you have your paperwork in order in terms of your report cards? Social Security cards? Birth certificates? Some of this may be needed for applications to college and even some scholarships need proof of your age or US citizenship.

- **Obstacles:** Have you had to overcome any? This is not to say "feel sorry for me" but to let them know that you had an obstacle and overcame it.

Once you have worked on defining yourself, it is best to keep everything in order. It makes sense to invest in a three-ring binder to hold all of your paperwork. We will review this in detail later in this chapter.

Books

There is a long list of great books out there designed to help you find the scholarship money you need. Some books provide a comprehensive list of just about every available scholarship you could imagine. Other books offer helpful tips on filling out the necessary scholarship forms. You may find books at your local library, your local bookstore, or on the internet. Many of these scholarships are short-lived, but there are quite a few that have been around a long time. There are even some that come and go, and come back again, depending on the available funds. Just remember: Do not give up.

Let us take a look at a few that you might find most useful for offering advice on scholarships, grants, and other topics, all of which can be purchased at **www.amazon.com**.

- *The Scholarship & Financial Aid Solution 2nd Edition; How to Go to College for Next to Nothing* (paperback) Shortcuts and tips with definitions, how to find scholarships, help with applications (filling them out, essays, interviews, what they look for, etc.), and follow up.

- *The Scholarship Book 13th Edition: The Complete Guide to Private-Sector Scholarships, Fellowships, Grants, and Loans for the Undergraduate* (paperback) — An acclaimed guide to private-sector scholarships, grants, and loans.

- *The College Board Scholarship Handbook 2016* (paperback) — Facts about more than 2,100 scholarship, internship, and loan programs offered to undergraduates by foundations, charitable organizations, and state and federal government agencies.

- *The College Board Getting Financial Aid* 2015 (paperback) — Gives you the "financial aid picture" for each of more than 3,000 colleges, universities, and technical schools.

- *Kaplan Scholarships 2016: Billions of Dollars in Free Money for College* (paperback) —Features information on programs that offer significant and unrestricted scholarships combined with tips and advice on how to get them.

- *Scholarships, Grants and Prizes 2016 (Peterson's Scholarships, Grants & Prizes)* (paperback) — Provides up-to-date details on millions of privately funded awards valued at billions of dollars.

- *America's Best Value Colleges, 2008 Edition (College Admissions Guides)* (paperback) — Profiles 150 schools that have low to moderate tuition rates and that are likely to help students by providing financial aid, scholarships, and grants.

- *Get Into Any College: Secrets of Harvard Students (Get Into Any College)* (paperback) — A book of strategy to help you get into the college that you want.

- US *News Ultimate College Guide 2011*(paperback) — Featuring complete data on more than 1,400 colleges and universities.

- *Fiske Guide to Colleges 2016* (paperback) — A leading guide to more than 300 colleges and universities.

- *The Big Book of Colleges 2012* (paperback) — Ranks 201 schools in 20 different categories.

Internet

You can also explore websites to find out even more information about schools, or to supplement your other resources. The internet is easy to use, and the information that you find is free.

Before we look at a few great sites, let us cover a few tips for effective internet scholarship searches and look at what you should watch out for.

- **Use your list:** Gather some of your thoughts from your work on "Defining Yourself" earlier in this chapter. Use those character descriptions to help you search for a scholarship, such as "high GPA" and extracurricular and community service activities.

- **Be specific:** When doing an internet search it can be more effective to enter a few words on the search bar rather than just one. For instance, if you are searching for a scholarship for biology majors, type "biology majors scholarships." Be specific in your search.

- **Use different search engines:** While many people use Google, there are other search engines that may provide you with different results, such as Dogpile, Yahoo, and Bing.

- **Advanced searches:** Some search engines, like Google, offer advanced search preferences, which you may want to check out. (They are usually located next to the search bar.)

- **Watch out for scams:** Be careful of application fees or requests for personal information. Just because something is on the internet does not mean it is legitimate. Watch out for identity theft and financial theft.

- **Do not use paid services:** Why pay for a search when you can find the information yourself? Often, paid searches are not legit. You may be paying for information that you can easily find elsewhere, not "insider information."

- **Make sure they are authentic:** Some sites say they "guarantee" scholarships, but that is not realistic. No one can guarantee you a scholarship. Some sites have only an email address and no phone number. That should concern you. A legitimate business would most likely offer a phone number as well as a website address and email.

According to the Federal Trade Commission, you should be on the alert for scholarship scams. The FTC cautions students to look for telltale lines:

- "The scholarship is guaranteed or your money back."
- "You cannot get this information anywhere else."
- "I just need your credit card or bank account number to hold this scholarship."
- "We will do all the work."
- "The scholarship will cost some money."
- "You have been selected by a 'national foundation' to receive a scholarship" or "You are a finalist" in a contest you never entered.

According to FinAid, the scams are vast and costly:

"Every year, several hundred thousand students and parents are defrauded by scholarship scams. The victims of these scams lose more than $100 million annually. Scam operations often imitate legitimate government agencies, grant-giving foundations, education lenders, and scholarship matching services, using official-sounding names containing words like 'National,' 'Federal,' 'Foundation,' or 'Administration.'"

Finaid.org offers helpful information about scholarship scams and what to watch out for at **www.finaid.org/scholarships/scams.phtml**. The topics cover:

- Common scholarship scams
- Protecting yourself from scholarship scams
- Evaluating scholarship matching services
- Evaluating financial aid consultants
- How to report scams
- Consumer education materials
- How to investigate suspicious offers
- The College Scholarship Fraud Prevention Act of 2000

Now let us review a few helpful sites for finding scholarships. Although there are more sites out there, with this list you should be able to access most private scholarships.

- **www.collegeboard.org** — Scholarship Search will find potential opportunities from a database of more than 2,300 sources of college funding, totaling nearly $3 billion in available aid.

- **www.collegenet.com** — Looks for scholarships that match your personal profile or keywords.

- **www.collegescholarships.com** — Scholarships are grouped by interest, and include middle school and high school awards.

- **www.collegeview.com** — Has been helping parents and students find scholarships and free money for college since 2001.

- **www.ed.gov** — Scholarships are searched by category, such as music and sports, as well as other personal information.

- **www.fastweb.com** — Personalized matching of scholarships to your unique profile.

- **www.internationalscholarships.com** — A resource for financial aid, college scholarships, and international scholarships for students wishing to study abroad.

- **http://offers.military.com/v/scholarships/flow** — Find millions of dollars in scholarships and grants exclusively for the military community.

- **www.salliemae.com** — During the 2007–2008 academic year, $2.5 million in need-based college scholarships were awarded to more than 1,000 students nationwide.

- **www.scholarships.com** — A plethora of scholarships, both state and national.

- **http://scholarships.fatomei.com** — Competitive and prestigious scholarships, fellowship and internship awards for college study, graduate school, and postgraduate research.

Colleges

While there are private scholarships awarded from various sources, some colleges and universities award scholarships directly to students with high GPAs and low income, or students that excel at sports, or for other reasons. You should always check at the school you are interested in attending to see if they have any direct scholarships that you can apply to receive. Some schools offer search engines directly on their sites for other scholarships as well. More and more scholarships are being added all the time. For instance, Harvard University provided $90 million in scholarships for undergraduate students during the 2006-2007 academic year.

According to their website at **www.harvard.edu**, 70 percent of students receive some form of aid, 100 percent of students can graduate debt-free, and 20 percent of students' families pay nothing. All of their scholarships are based on financial need. A growing number of Ivy League colleges (with Princeton leading them in being the first) do not let students 'borrow' to graduate. They have assistance on a need basis, as they want to have all of their students graduating debt free.

Let us look at a few of the college scholarships that you can receive nationwide. Keep in mind that each school offers many more scholarships than what is shown below, so check the websites for more.

The University of Minnesota

The University of Minnesota offers, among many other scholarships, the Maroon and Gold Leadership Award of $12,000 per year for four years. To be eligible, you must be a Minnesota resident and be in the top five percent of your graduating class. You must have outstanding academic performance, demonstrated leadership, creativity, and community involvement. You may find out about other scholarships offered and apply online at: **http://admissions.tc.umn.edu/costsaid/ schol_campus.html**, or contact:

> University of Minnesota
> Office of Admissions
> 240 Williamson Hall
> 231 Pillsbury Drive S.E.
> Minneapolis, MN 55455-0213
> 612-625-5000

New York University

New York University offers the Helene Fuld Scholarships for entering freshmen in the 15-month Accelerated Baccalaureate Degree for nursing students. Students with an exceptional background in the sciences are eligible for $10,000 divided equally over the four semesters. The selection process is highly competitive, and only eight students are selected in both the fall and spring semesters. You may find out more about this and other scholarships and apply online at: **www.nyu.edu/admissions/ undergraduate-admissions/financial-aid.html**, or contact:

> New York University
> Undergraduate Admissions Processing Center
> 22 Washington Square North
> New York, NY 10011
> 212-998-4500

UC San Diego

UC San Diego offers a variety of scholarships, including Freshmen Merit Scholarships, of which you can qualify for two of them. You may find out more at: **www.ucsd.edu,** or contact:

> University of California, San Diego
> 9500 Gilman Dr.
> La Jolla, CA 92093
> 858-534-2230

Boston College

Boston College offers millions of dollars for need-based scholarships. Many are donor-established funds. Boston also has other need-based Grants as well.

For more information, visit **www.bc.edu/admission/undergrad** or contact:

> Boston College
> Office of Undergraduate Admission
> Devlin Hall 208
> 140 Commonwealth Avenue
> Chestnut Hill, MA 02467-3809
> 617-552-3100 or (800) 360-2522

Many colleges have automatic Freshmen Merit scholarships, contingent on several factors. Usually GPA and SAT/ACT scores are the main eligibility requirements. Other colleges also have Presidential Scholarships or Honors College awards as well. You need to go to their website to research this and call their financial aid department.

Local Organizations

We have examined some of the scholarships you can find from private sources and from the schools themselves, but there are still other places to hunt for "free money" for college. Local organizations, such as the Rotary club, the Kiwanis, VFW, American Legion, Lion's Club, Elks Club, Retired Teachers funds, and other local groups and organizations sometimes have college scholarships available. Why? The local organizations and clubs make scholarships part of their commitment to serve their communities.

So how do you go about finding these scholarships? Many of these scholarships are posted as announcements in local newspapers, either in the form of ads, articles, or classifieds. The announcements provide you with information on how to go about applying, who might be eligible, and the scholarship amount. If you do not see an announcement for a scholarship in the newspaper, you can check the organization's website to see if scholarships are listed. For instance, the Rotary Club of Los Angeles offers awards of approximately $166,000 per year to 77 local students to assist them toward degreed studies. According to the Club:

> "There are four types of scholarships for graduating high school seniors — Close Family College Scholarships, Courtland H. and Edna Hurlock Barr College Scholarships, LA5 College Scholarships, and Past Presidents' Technical Education Scholarships.

> "All scholarships are awarded based on academic achievement, financial need, community and school service, and personal qualities and strengths. A committee of LA5 members makes the final selection. Each college scholarship will be renewed only if the recipient meets the grade point average requirement and remains enrolled as a full-time student with a minimum of 12 units for the coming academic year."

You can find out more about the Rotary Club of Los Angeles scholarships at:

> 900 Wilshire Blvd. Suite 418
> Los Angeles, CA 90017
> **www.rotaryla5.org**
> 213-624-8601

You might not live in a big city like Los Angeles, but some Rotary clubs in smaller towns offer scholarships. Take, for instance, the Rotary Club of North Colorado Springs. They award need-based scholarships of up to $10,000 to help cover expenses for the first two years of college. Three to four awards are generally awarded per year.

> Rotary Club of North Colorado Springs
> P.O. Box 7056
> Colorado Springs, CO 80933
> **www.northcoloradospringsrotary.org**

Kiwanis, Lion's Clubs, and the VFW are other great avenues to check for scholarship funds. While the scholarships may not pay your entire way through college — some of the scholarships are as small as $500 — remember the idea is to apply for as many scholarships as you can to get as much funding as you can, and all of these small scholarships can add up to a large amount. Let us take a look at a few other scholarships that are offered by these local organizations throughout the nation. These are meant to give you an idea of what is available. Be sure to check the local organizations in your area. You may find that several of them offer scholarships that can help you shave thousands off your college expenses.

Keep in mind that these are to give you an idea of what is out there. You should always check local organizations in your area.

The Ocala Silver Springs Rotary Club in Marion County, Florida offers four $1,000 scholarships to their high school seniors, based on "Service Above Self." They drop off these applications at schools or send to the senior guidance counselors by email.

The Kiwanis Club of Issaquah, Washington offers scholarships to one graduating senior from three local schools. The scholarships are each a $1,000 cash award used to further the student's education. According to the club, eligibility requirements include:

- Applicant will have participated in school and community activities that demonstrate outstanding community service.
- Applicant will have demonstrated academic success.

> Kiwanis Club of Issaquah
> P.O. Box 1111
> Issaquah, WA 98027
> 425-392-4016
> info@issaquah.kiwanis.org
> **www.issaquahkiwanis.org**

Unlike some scholarships, neither the Kiwanis Club of Issaquah's scholarship or the Ocala Silver Springs Rotary Club are need-based. Instead, the scholarships consider your community service experience.

Some local organizations sponsor scholarships for students who are attending a certain school, such as this one sponsored by the Lion's Club in Fairbanks, Alaska:

The Fairbanks Host Lions Club offers $1,000 to students from the Fairbanks North Star Borough who are attending the University of Alaska Fairbanks, and have been employed while attending school.

UAF Advancement Services
4001 Geist Road Suite 6 • P.O. Box 757530
University of Alaska Fairbanks
Fairbanks, AK 99775
907-474-640
www.uaf.edu

The VFW is also a wonderful organization to check for scholarships. They offer two scholarships programs, the Voice of Democracy Scholarship Competition and the Patriot's Pen Essay Contest (for middle school-aged children).

Created in 1947, the Voice of Democracy (VOD) scholarship program is an audio-essay contest for high school students in grades 9-12 that annually provides more than $3 million in scholarships. The first-place winner, who competes with all the first-place VFW Department winners, receives a $30,000 scholarship that is paid directly to the recipient's American university, college, or vocational/technical school.

Patriot's Pen, a youth essay writing contest endorsed by the National Association of Secondary School Principals' contest criteria, is a nationwide competition that gives students in grades six, seven, and eight the opportunity to write essays expressing their views on democracy. Annually, more than 115,000 students participate in the contest.

Contestants write a 300 to 400-word essay based on an annual patriotic theme. The first-place winner receives a $10,000 savings bond and an all-expense-paid trip to Washington D.C. The top national winners each receive a savings bond anywhere from $1,000 to $10,000.

The VFW also awards military scholarships designed to help with education and training. The scholarships provide 25 VFW members with $3,000 scholarships annually. Members must be currently serving in uniform or have been discharged within the 36 months before the Dec. 31 deadline. The VFW also offers the Scout of the Year Scholarship program that provides a $5,000 award to an outstanding scout. Scouts must be recipient of a Boy Scout Eagle Award, a Venture Scouting Silver Award, or a Sea Scout Quartermaster Award.

To find out about eligibility requirements and how to apply, contact:

> VFW
> General Info 816-756-3390
> info@vfw.org
> **www.vfw.org**

The Retired Teachers are nonprofit organizations that look out for the interests of teachers, as well as making a mark in the community with volunteer services and other community work. Some of the associations offer scholarships to the students in the community. In some states, they have local scholarships and then they can advance to state level for even more money. You need to check your state's Retired Teachers Association to see if there are scholarships available. Most offer scholarships specifically to those studying teaching.

Contact information varies by state. However, the AARP offers a list of state RTA websites at: **www.aarp.org/about-aarp/nrt**a.

Let us take a look at an example of a scholarship offered by an RTA:

The California Retired Teachers Association offers the Laura E. Settle Foundation. According to the association:

> "The program is administered through the financial aid offices of 31 participating University of California and California State University campuses. Scholarships are awarded to students in their junior, senior, or graduate years in an accredited teaching program. The LES Foundation provides $2,000 scholarships to 31 students annually. Another 13 $300 grants from the affiliated Outler fund are also awarded to teachers who plan on working in elementary schools."

> California Retired Teachers Association
> 800 Howe Avenue, #370
> Sacramento, CA 95825
> 800-523-2782
> 916-923-2200
> **www.calrta.org**

Again, check with you own state's Retired Teachers Association to see if you might be eligible for a scholarship. Remember that each one may have different criteria.

Scholarships for Specific Groups

As we have learned previously, scholarship awards are based on multiple reasons, including need, merit, and those who might be star athletes. However, there are also scholarships created for specific groups, such as minorities and single parents, as well as those that have special interests or are studying a specific field. Many of these scholarships bring diversity to a school or a field of study. For instance, a local engineering group may want to bring more women into the field, so they may offer scholarships for women who are studying engineering. To find scholarships for specific groups, check community service organizations and clubs that pertain to your field of study in your area.

Here are a few scholarships that are examples of special interests and course of studies:

The Vegetarian Resource Group

The Vegetarian Resource Group offers two $5,000 college scholarships. According to the group:

> "Due to the generosity of an anonymous donor, the Vegetarian Resource Group each year will award one $10,000 scholarship and two $5,000 scholarships to US high school students who have promoted vegetarianism in their schools and/or communities. Vegetarians do not eat meat, fish, or fowl. Two awards of $5,000 each will be given…

Applicants will be judged on having shown compassion, courage, and a strong commitment to promoting a peaceful world through a vegetarian diet/lifestyle. Payment will be made to the student's college (U.S.-based only). Winners of the scholarships give permission to release their names to the media. Applications and essays become property of the Vegetarian Resource Group. We may ask finalists for more information."

The Vegetarian Resource Group
P.O. Box 1463, Baltimore, MD 21203
410-366-8343
Email: vrg@vrg.org
www.vrg.org/student/scholar.htm

The NCCPAP/AICPA Scholarships

The National Conference of CPA Practitioners (NCCPAP) and the AICPA have teamed together to offer scholarships to graduating high school seniors planning to pursue careers as certified public accountants. Merit-based scholarships of $1,000 each are awarded. There are several other scholarships on their website as well.

To apply, the student must be a graduating high school senior with a grade point average of at least 3.3 on a 4.0 scale. The applicant must have applied to or have been accepted at a two- or four-year college and be enrolled as a full-time student. Awards are made for the academic year following application and are sent directly to the school for credit to the account of the student recipient.

NCCPAP/AICPA Scholarships

888-488-5400

Email: lanak.ncCPAp@verizon.net

To look for specific groups scholarships:

- First, make a list of all of your interests and your field of study and search local organizations affiliated with it to see if they offer grants or scholarships. Information is often available on their websites.

- Next, check with your school's financial aid office. There may be a scholarship sponsored by alumni groups or in honor of someone affiliated with the school.

- If you are a senior in high school, check with your guidance counselor (as many scholarships are sent directly to them) or scholarship coordinator if you have one. If they are unaware of local scholarships, go to the main Guidance and Testing department or to your school board.

- Also search for scholarships on databases, such as www.fastweb.com and www.gocollege.com. Other potential sources have been listed in this book.

- Do not forget to check local papers. Sometimes the organizations have postings, articles, or ads about their scholarships.

- If there is no website for the organization, try making a phone call to them.

- Look at all your options. Search for all available funding. Do not limit yourself in your search.

Keeping Track of It All

When you are applying for scholarships, you may be asked for the same information again and again, so it is best to keep a file with important documents that you might need to fill out your scholarship application. This also ends up helping to make the process of applying easier for each one, as you are using the same data, sometimes just put down in a different order. Equally important is keeping track of where you applied and whom you applied with. Here are some ideas for keeping track of your important application documents:

- **Purchase a three-ring binder:** You can use a three-ring binder to hold your paperwork and place tabs between the scholarships that you applied for. You can keep copies of all of your important documents in the side folders.

- **Make copies of paperwork:** In the binder, you might want to have the name and address of your school, as well as your own personal contact information, along with letters of recommendations and your essays — which you will learn more about in Chapter 8.

- **Document fees:** If you pay any fees at all, make sure you keep a copy of the check that you submitted. That way you will know how much you sent and when you sent it in case the check gets lost or misplaced.

- **Write everything down:** Make a note of what scholarships you applied for, the date you applied for each one, what you submitted to each, and where you found out about them. Again, make a copy of everything you submit. If you keep copies of your work on your computer, back it up with a flash drive, an internal drive, or even on a second computer, as all of these are liable to either crash or break.

- **Make a calendar:** Keep a calendar handy to make note of when you applied for each scholarship and when the deadline for applying is.

- **Follow up:** Keep a list of all paperwork that you have to follow up on and when it needs to be done by. You can also mark the dates for follow-up in your calendar.

- **Bookmark pages:** Make sure you bookmark the websites that you found the scholarships on. It makes it easier to backtrack.

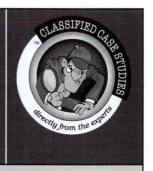

CASE STUDY: PAUL HOLSTEIN, Founder of LifeOrganizers.com and Vice President of CableOrganizer.com

I have found that life is best when it's organized, so I created **Lifeorganizers.com**, a growing collection of resources for managing time, home, family, career, and finances, along with a segment dedicated to college students.

How do you overcome college clutter crisis?

My personal motto is "Handle it, file it, delegate it, or throw it away." An easy technique to help you deal with paper and desk clutter is to "handle it" by dealing with it now rather than letting it accumulate and morph into a pile of clutter on your desk. Whatever comes through your inbox, email, mail box, voice mail, cellphone text messages, and even items in your wallet — handle it first by opening it and deciding on what needs to be done with the item. Either you will find a place for it by filing it for reference later, delegate it to the relevant party, or throw it away.

How do you choose the best filing system for you?

Every piece of paper should have a place where it can be filed out of sight and found easily when needed. A few filing solutions that fit perfectly into small spaces and dorm rooms are a two-drawer filing cabinet, accordion file folders, and notebooks with built-in filing pockets. Plastic file boxes work great too because they are available in a range of colors and patterns which are not only portable but can be stashed under your bed when not in use. Choose a system that lets you be flexible. You can file according to date, semester, courses, alphabetically, or you can even divide your drawer into two sections, one marked as "reference" for papers needed rarely, and the second as a "projects/course work" section for documents referred to most often. Do not forget to make a "finance and budget" section with folders to store your receipts and bills either by month or by the type of purchase.

How do you handle email clutter?

Keeping like emails together will save you endless frustration when you need to access information quickly. Create folders in your email application to store emails by theme or subject. You can have a social folder to keep track of your friends and activities and a coursework folder to store lecture notes or class venue changes.

Outlook and most major email applications let you create folders and "rules" to route emails directly into their predestined folders according to your preferences.

How do you handle cable clutter?

You likely use your computer for college, social networking, downloading music, charging your cellphone, gaming, and more, resulting in a lot of peripheral wires cluttering your workspace. There are a variety of products that can help ensure that the cables behind your PC do not become a trip hazard or dust collector. Try bundling your cables using cable ties or shortening their lengths using cable turtles. You may also want to hide them using braided sleeving or make them safer for foot traffic using cord covers. Find out more at **www.CableOrganizer.com**.

Wrapping It Up

Getting a scholarship will take some time and effort, but the end results are worth it. Keep in mind that you should start planning and applying for scholarships early. Apply for every scholarship that you qualify for. There are numerous places to look for scholarships. Do not just look at one website or in one book. Do not limit yourself with the types of scholarships that you think you are eligible to receive. For instance, do not assume that just because you are a minority that you should only look at minority scholarships. Or that because you have chosen a particular major, that those are the only ones to apply for, as there are quite a few scholarships that are for any major.

Keep your options open. Make sure that you keep your scholarship paperwork orderly as you most likely will be using the same information for other applications. Be sure to make copies, and keep track of everything you send in and when everything is due. You do not want to miss a deadline when it comes to your applications. If time becomes a problem, focus first on the local or state-level scholarships before you work on the national ones. In this day and age, national scholarships with online applications have been known to receive hundreds of thousands of applications. At the same time, the more difficult the application, the fewer people that will apply. Although it takes some effort and time to garner a scholarship, it will reduce the amount you have to take out in student loans. Your bank account will thank you.

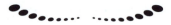

Chapter 8

Bringing It Home

The previous chapter explored the types of scholarships that are available and where to find them. We will now concentrate on how to win those scholarships. There are specific things you can do to increase the likelihood of receiving a scholarship, including filling out your application correctly, writing a winning essay, making sure your transcripts are in order, and successfully making it through an interview. By making sure that you do it all the right way, you will increase your odds of winning a scholarship and bringing the money home.

How to Win the Dream Scholarship

Like pursuing any of your dreams, it takes time, effort, and planning to win a dream scholarship. Free money does not fall out of the sky. You need to work for it and do the right things to increase the odds of getting it. So where do you start?

- **Keep your information in a safe spot.** Once you have thoroughly researched the many scholarships that you can apply for, gather the paperwork necessary to complete them. Keep it all in a safe spot. Chapter 7 offers helpful tips on keeping track of it all.

- **Know your deadlines.** Make sure you know the deadlines and apply for each scholarship as early as you can. There is no sense in sending in your information if the deadline has come and gone. If you are unsure about whether the deadline is for mailing date or receipt date, make sure that you send it early enough to be received by the listed date. When mailing, it can take up to seven days to get somewhere, even in the same town. If submitting electronically, do not wait until the last minute in case there is a problem with either your computer or the server. Early is always better than late, as late can disqualify you.

- **Keep track of fees.** There might be fees involved with photocopies, postage, and application fees, so make sure you keep track of money submitted by photocopying your check. (Read Chapter 9 for what to watch out for in fees — you need to be careful for scams.) Fees are unusual or normally minimal, but do your research before paying.

- **Read the fine print.** Before sending in your forms, read all the fine print to make sure that you have covered everything and followed ALL directions.

- **Double-check everything.** Check your application, essay, or other paperwork for grammatical errors, content errors, and typos before you send it in. Do not rely on spell check! Double-check to make sure you have submitted everything and placed it in the correct order if specified.

- **Do not leave spaces blank.** Instead, write N/A or 0.

- **Make sure you (or your counselor or parent) sign the form,** if it is requested.

- **Only include what is requested.** Do not send in what was not required, like a résumé (most of what goes on an application is on your résumé, so it is only repeating it) or extra letters of recommendations.

- **Look for scholarships every year.** There are usually new ones available.

Now that we have covered a few of the basics, we will go over what might be requested for your scholarship and how to make sure you have covered everything effectively.

Recommendations

Often scholarship applications require letters of recommendations. Even if they do not, it is a good idea to have a few in your pocket, as you never know when you will need one. They come in handy in all kinds of situations, like college admission and job recommendations. You may need three to four letters of recommendation from different sources just for one scholarship application.

A letter of academic recommendation is most effective when it includes specific information:

- **The letter should be written on letterhead.** For instance, if your boss is writing the letter, it should be written on the company's stationary with the name of the company and the address shown. Your counselor or teachers should use letterhead as well. It is not only more authentic but more professional.

- **The letter should include brief background information about who is writing the letter.** Are they your boss? Co-worker? The letter needs to state their background and their relationship to you.

- **The letter should include the title of the person who is writing the letter.** Are they president of a company? Instructor from a school? Make sure they sign the document with their title below their signature.

- The content of the letter should also:

    ⇥ Contain information about how long the person has known you and in what capacity
    ⇥ Provide testimony to your aptitude, attitude, and industriousness
    ⇥ Compliment your character, praise your leadership skills, and make mention of your team player approach
    ⇥ Explain why you are deserving of the scholarship

- If the letter is a character reference, generally written by people who know you well, then the letter can include the following:

    ⇥ Stories of hard work that you have done
    ⇥ Mentions of your accomplishments
    ⇥ Information about memberships or organizations that you belong to and what you have done for the organization
    ⇥ Discussion about your personal attributes and strengths

These things can also be included in letters from the others as well, as long as you tell them about it. That is why giving a résumé to someone writing the letter is always a good idea.

If you are wondering whom you should ask for a letter of recommendation, here are a few ideas:

- Someone who is experienced with your work or efforts
- Someone who can articulately compose a letter (very important, as some people just cannot write very well)
- Someone who has a high title, such as your guidance counselor, principal, a president of a company, a doctor, lawyer, or minister.
- Someone who would not hesitate to write you a letter of recommendation

Do not ask for a letter from someone who is related to you. A few ideas for sources of letters are:

- Your employer or immediate supervisor
- A coworker that holds a higher position
- Your coach, especially if you are applying for sports scholarships
- The principal or dean or guidance counselor of your school
- The head of an organization that you volunteered your time with
- The sponsor of a club that you belong to
- Someone who is familiar with any community service you may be involved with

While it is sometimes a little unnerving to ask someone to write a letter of recommendation for you, there are a few ways that you can make the process easier.

- Timing is important. Make sure you ask at a good time. For instance, do not ask your boss to write a letter or recommendation when there is a pile of work to do and it is 30 minutes to closing.

- Explain why you want the letter. What is the letter's purpose? To get into school? For a scholarship?

- Be specific about what you need in the letter and when you need it by. Give them a due date.

- Supply the letter writer with information about whom the letter should be addressed to.

- You might want to explain to the person writing what the letter should cover, such as work habits, length of time that you were employed, and so on. Have the information ready for them. Provide them with a résumé so that they can write a well-rounded letter.

- You may offer to outline a letter for the person in order to make it easier for them.

- Give them some notice to write it, at least a week, if not two. Nobody likes having to do something at the last minute. It never hurts to gently remind them a couple of days ahead of time.

- Try to make the process as easy as you can for the person writing the letter.

Do not forget to:

- Double-check the letter for typos
- Make sure it is signed
- Make sure it addresses what needs to be addressed
- Make yourself a few copies

- Make sure you enclose it with your other scholarship application materials
- Thank the person for writing the letter

The Essay

Of course, many scholarships ask for more than just letters of recommendation. Most ask that you write an essay (even if it is only one paragraph). Others want to interview you as well — both of which we will explore in this chapter. Essays allow you to show off your grammatical and writing skills, as well as allow you to show off your point of view and how well you can persuade or argue a point. Writing excellent scholarship essays are important to winning the scholarship, so we will cover this in detail.

When writing an essay, consider the following:

- **Read the directions.** It is vital that you read the directions carefully to make sure you know what your essay is supposed to cover. You might want to read the directions twice just to make sure you understand what is expected of you.

- **Make sure your essay is the right length.** Often the directions will give you a word count. Make sure you do not go higher or lower than the word count to any large degree.

- **Meet the deadline.** Do not miss the deadline, or you will miss the scholarship opportunity.

- **Organize your thoughts.** Write an introduction to what you want to say, write the contents, and include a summary of what you said. Essays need to be organized and easy to follow.

- **Look it over.** Has your essay addressed the topic or answered the question that was asked? Does your essay flow? Is your essay easy to read? Does it make sense?

- **Make it interesting.** You want to write something that others want to read. This is no time to be dull! Think of an interesting and compelling topic if given a choice, or a captivating way to address their topic, and how it applies to your experiences and/or field of study if possible.

- **Keep it focused on you, unless otherwise stated.** You are "selling" yourself to the scholarship provider. The essay needs to focus on your strong attributes.

- **Back up what you are saying.** Make sure you are properly referencing your statements. If you are quoting someone, make sure to use proper quotes.

- **Do not steal ideas.** Come up with your own thoughts. This is your chance to shine.

- **Write a rough draft and a final draft.** The more drafts, the better it will be. Do not be too afraid or lazy to rework what you wrote. Good writing takes time and effort.

- **Have someone else look at it.** Get feedback from someone you trust. Ask a writing or English teacher to look it over. Ask your parents. Ask a friend. Do not assume everything is perfect.

- **Double-check it.** Make sure you do not have any typos or grammatical errors.

- **Make sure you have addressed what was asked.** Once you are finished with your essay, go back and read the directions. Ask yourself again if you have covered what was asked.

- **Consider the judges or organization.** If you are writing an essay for example for the VFW, remember they are elderly patriotic people. If it is an organization that believes in a particular charity and you have experience with that charity, then do not leave that out. Always consider the audience.

- **Make copies.** Do not forget to make copies of your essay. Keep your paperwork in a safe place with all of your other materials, as presented in Chapter 7.

- **Mail it.** Make sure you include your essay with your other materials when you send it off. Do not miss your deadline!

Some scholarships will choose a topic for you. For instance, for a science scholarship, you may be asked to write about something in the science field. However, some scholarships will ask you to choose a topic. If you are choosing your own topic, be sure to pick a good, strong topic that means something to you. You will have a better chance of writing an effective essay if you believe in what you are saying. You might consider writing about something that not only interests you but also gives insight to the scholarship committee as to what kind of person you are. For instance, if you are applying for a teaching scholarship, you might choose a scholarship topic (if given a choice) on working with students with disabilities. That would give the scholarship committee a feeling that you are concerned with students who may be struggling. Some will just ask a question of or about you. Just make sure that you answer the question and back up your answer with good reasons as well.

Make sure you grab their attention in the first or second sentence. The beginning of your essay should try to capture the audience and make them want to read more. You also need to stay somewhat focused in your thoughts. Keep the angle of your topic narrow; it will be easier to write something interesting and get into the topic more deeply. Plus, your thoughts will not seem too scattered.

Be honest. Do not make up things to impress people. Be yourself. If you have had any obstacles in your life, this is the time to tell about them. If possible, relate them to the topic or question. Remember, you are not asking for pity but letting them know what you have gone through and what you have done to not let it get in your way.

You can get help with writing your essay on different websites. For instance, at www.collegeboard.org, you can find sample essays, as well as pointers for drafting your own essay and responding to questions. There are also services available to help you write an essay. Cambridge Essay Service can look over your essay and offer advice for making it better. You can contact them at:

Cambridge Essay Service
617-354-2242
sandy413@yahoo.com
www.hbsguru.com

Or try:

> **www.essayedge.com**
> 888-GET-AN-EDGE

You can also order a kit to assist you with essays and letters of recommendations:

> College Admission Essay Toolkit:
> **http://instantcollegeadmissionessay.com**

> Instant Recommendation Letter Kit:
> **http://instantrecommendationletterkit.com**

There are also quite a few professional writing services available that you can find in your area. You could start by looking at professional résumé-writing services. No doubt, they could help you on your essay should you need it. Just make sure that when you send in your essay to the scholarship committee that it is as good as it can be. The potential for scholarship dollars greatly increases with a good, well-written essay.

Filling Out the Application

Along with the essay, you may also be filling out an application. Filling out an application correctly is important for scholarships, grants, college entrance, and beyond. No matter what the application is for, it is important to fill it out completely. While some applications are filled out online, others are not. Regardless, there are things to keep in mind:

- **Make note of the deadline:** First of all, you should read the deadline for the application. Make sure you still have time to turn it in. Make note of the deadline and get the application in as far in advance as you can.

- **Read the application carefully:** Next, read through the application. Read all of the fine print. Make sure that you meet the eligibility requirements and that you understand what needs to be done.

- **Ask questions if in doubt:** If you have questions, you may want to ask at the source, if possible. Do not make assumptions. Many times applications have contact numbers or email in case of questions.

- **Make a copy before you fill it in:** Make a copy of the application, and fill out a draft first. You do not want your application to look messy or have something crossed out. Always type or fill out on the computer if possible. They look much neater than hand-written ones.

- **If you have to fill out the form by hand, use the right pen:** Make sure you use a black or blue pen (unless otherwise specified) to fill out the form.

- **See what is requested:** Find out what other paperwork the application is requesting, such as transcripts, a personal statement (see below), or letters of recommendation. Gather them together, and do not forget to send them in with the application. If submitting online, check what needs to be uploaded and what might need to be mailed. If the letter is supposed to be uploaded by the recommender, remind them a couple of days of ahead of time as well.

- **Look for fees:** Check to see if there is any kind of fee. If there is, make sure it is enclosed. They may request that you send a money order or cashier's check. If they request that, do not send in a personal check. Read Chapter 9 about scholarship scams to watch out for when sending in any money or personal information. As stated before, not many have fees. The ones that usually do are the scholarships for the arts, or a few with small fees for paperwork and processing.

- **Make a copy of the finished application:** After you have finished filling out your application, be sure to make a copy that you keep on file. Make a copy of the letters of recommendation and essay as well.

Personal Statement

If your application requires a personal statement — perhaps in addition to an essay or in place of one — it is important to give the scholarship committee a sense of who you are. Follow the directions on the statement request. However, if there are no directions or if they are general in nature, keep the following in mind:

- Give a sense of who you are.
- State your qualifications for receiving the scholarship.
- State how the scholarship could help you reach your goals.
- State what your long-term academic and career goals are.
- When asked why you deserve the scholarship, you can say why you need it or that it would be an honor, or what great help it would be to win it, rather than saying, "I deserve this scholarship because…"

A personal statement should always:

- Address what was asked in the directions.
- Be free of typos and grammatical errors.
- Make sense from sentence to sentence and paragraph to paragraph.

- Concentrate on a main topic. Stay on track of what was asked. Do not wander far with your thoughts.

- Make sure your name and contact information appears on each page. That way if the paper gets misplaced or lost, it can be returned to your pile of paperwork.

- Offer a sense of who you are. If you are a leader, then you want the essay to reflect your leadership qualities.

- Some of the most common essay questions: What are your education and career goals? How can one person make a difference? Why do you need this scholarship? What person or event has impacted your life and how?

Every application is different. You may not be asked for a personal statement. If you are, make sure that you follow the guidelines for what the scholarship is requesting for a personal statement. They may ask about your career goals or where the scholarship funds will go. They may want a few words, a few paragraphs, or a few pages. It may be as extensive as an essay or as simple as a few sentences. Always read and follow the directions closely with each application.

Awards and Achievements

Some scholarships also request information about your awards or achievements. If you have a paper copy, such as a copy of an award that you received for community service work, you might want to send it in along with mentioning it on the application. Make sure that the application does not say anything about enclosing any extra paperwork. Put the application guidelines ahead of everything else. Other achievements you have earned may include things noted in your transcripts. For instance, your GPA will be shown, but it does not hurt to mention a high GPA on your application if there is a place for it.

Keep in mind the following when it comes to awards and achievements:

- Include mention of the awards or achievements that help demonstrate your leadership skills, your willingness to work as a team player, your volunteer work, or other areas that could help shape your character. Whether it is academic, athletic, or community service awards, be sure to list them all.

- Do not mention something that is not applicable or is missing the mark. If you won an award for "Most Hot Dogs Eaten in 30 Minutes" or something that is irrelevant to your future schooling and career, it should not be included.

- Think about your high school years, as well as your early college years. You may have awards and achievements that have slipped your mind.

- If there is a way, try to connect your awards and achievements to how they are a good example for the scholarship. For instance, if you won a leadership award and you are studying business management, perhaps you can tie that into your personal statement somehow.

The Transcripts

As mentioned in Chapter 2, transcripts are required for college application requirements but can also be requested by scholarship and grant committees. Transcripts are important, as they contain a record of all courses, grades, and degrees — especially for merit-based work — but they are not all of your application materials. You impress a scholarship committee with more than just your grades. Your essay, application, personal statement, and letter of recommendation all factor in.

Transcripts are sent only at your request, so typically you have to sign a form that says you agree to release them and to where they will be released. A typical fee for transcripts is five dollars per copy of each official transcript that is sent out. Transcripts must be sent directly to the school or organization that is requesting them in order to be official. You can also request a copy for yourself, but they are considered "unofficial." It is a good idea to keep a copy of your transcripts on file for yourself, as you may need a copy to show at your scholarship interview. It is also a good idea to know what they look like.

You can generally request transcripts in several ways:

- By fax
- By mail or email
- In person

You can often request your transcripts online at your school. Normally there is a fee for transcripts, and many schools will not release them without pay. Generally, you must fax a signature page back to the school before they are released. If you have several schools to get your transcripts from, it may behoove you to do it all at once. Make a note of when you requested your transcripts. That way, if they do not arrive on time, you can call to find out if they were sent or got lost in the mail. There are transcript clearinghouses that you can also use, as was mentioned in Chapter 2, such as the National Student Clearinghouse.

> National Student Clearinghouse
> 13454 Sunrise Valley Drive, Suite 300
> Herndon, VA 20171
> 703-742-4200
> **www.studentclearinghouse.org.**

There are certain circumstances when transcripts will not be sent out, such as if a student has a hold on his or her records.

The Interview

Some scholarships, just like with college entrance requirements, request an interview. We will now examine the interview process and go over what is expected of you and how to make it smoother. Keep the information in mind for other interviews you may have — from job interviews to college entrance interviews — as the process is usually similar for each of these.

Some, but not all, scholarships require an interview. Often, the more competitive the scholarship is or the more prestigious the school awarding the scholarship is, the more rigorous the process is for getting the money. That may include an interview in person or by phone if you do not live near them. There are several ways in which to conduct an interview, and they can all vary in procedure. Some are more casual in nature with just one or two people in the room, or they could be more formal and extensive with a panel of members waiting their turn to ask you questions. A scholarship interview can be intimidating, but the better prepared you are, the less intimidating it will be.

How to prepare before the interview:

- Bring a copy of the paperwork: It is best to bring along a copy of all of your scholarship paperwork that was submitted to the scholarship committee, such as your essay, transcripts, and application. Just in case something is missing at your interview, you will have a copy on hand for them to refer to.

- Review materials: Review your scholarship materials before you have an interview. You may be applying for many scholarships, and you want to be sure that you are familiar with the one that you are dealing with at the moment. You do not want to get your information confused. Make sure you know what the essay topic or question was and how you answered it, what your personal statement covered, and your conclusion. Also, go over what you wrote for your awards and achievements.

- Re-read the original scholarship application request: Think about what the scholarship committee might be looking for in a candidate, and be prepared. Research the organization that is awarding the scholarship so that you know what they stand for and believe in. They may have a motto about themselves or donate to a particular charity. This can help in more than one way. You never know when they might ask a question to see if you know anything about them have an experience that relates to something they are passionate about. These things will help you stand out in a positive way in the interview.

- Make notes: Make notes to yourself about any details that could help you refresh your thoughts. Keep a copy on hand to review the day before the interview.

- Practice for your interview: Practice with family or friends. You could even videotape yourself to see how you spoke and how your body language was during a practice interview. Then go back and redo the run-through, making corrections and improvements.

- Know the location: Make sure you know where the interview is. Get your directions ahead of time. If you can, you might want to make the drive ahead of time to see exactly where it is and how long it takes you to get there. Never be late. It is always best to be a few minutes early. Leave early in case of heavy traffic or other unforeseen circumstances.

- Know where to park: If the interview paperwork does not state where to park, perhaps you can contact someone at the organization to ask where to park and if there are any parking fees. Bring money just in case you have to park somewhere with meters or other fees.

- Bring contact information with you: In case of an emergency, such as car trouble, you want to be able to call if there is a delay.

- Get a good night's rest the night before: It will keep you alert and refreshed.

- Eat beforehand: You do not want to think about hunger pangs during your interview or have your stomach growling. Make sure you eat a good meal before you go and bring along a snack, such as a granola bar, just in case you need an energy boost.

- Wear something professional: You do not need to go overboard, but dress nice. No jeans, tee-shirts, or flip flops.

- Arrive early: Ten to 15 minutes early is a good amount of time.

- Turn off your cellphone (or leave it in your car): Even when it is on vibrate it can still be heard.

During the interview:

- Do not forget to breathe deeply. It will relax you so you can concentrate on your thoughts.

- Always greet each interviewer with a firm handshake and hello.

- Make eye contact with your interviewers. When someone is speaking to you, look back at him or her.

- It never hurts to smile. Smiling shows off your personality.

- Sit up straight, and watch your body language. Do not slump or fidget.

- Listen carefully to the questions before you answer each.

- You do not have to rush your answers. You can take your time to formulate your thoughts. One good way to do this, especially if you have a ready answer, is to silently repeat the question to yourself.

- Do not give just a 'yes' or 'no' answer. Explain yourself. At the same time, do not go on and on either.

- Be honest. Lying is not going to get you anywhere except the rejection list.

- Show pride in your accomplishments. Do not be pompous and arrogant, but do not hide what you should show off.

- Ask for clarification if you do not understand something. It is okay to have the committee rephrase or restate something for you.

- If you do not know the answer to a question, you are better off telling them that you honestly do not know, rather than making something up.

- Do not be afraid to ask questions about the process, the scholarship, or anything else.

- Thank the interviewers for their time. They will appreciate it. If you can, send a note of thanks afterwards.

What might the interviewers ask? It is hard to say exactly what you will be asked during an interview, but hopefully the following will give you an idea of what kinds of questions and topics might be covered so you can be prepare for them.

- Your background: Where you were born and raised? What was your first job?

- You may be asked about your school records, your ranking, and what your GPA is.

- You may be asked about what classes you took previously and how they apply to your field of study.

- You may be asked if you have hobbies, pastimes, or do any volunteer work.

- You may be asked about your five-year goals, your 10-year goals, and your lifetime goals.

- You may be asked about your financial picture and how you plan to pay for schooling. Or if you plan on working at all.

- You may be asked about your family and who they are.

- You may be asked about where you plan to reside after college and what job you will be aiming for.

- You may be asked to role-play and answer questions as to what your reaction would be to "such and such," or what you would do in a particular situation.

- You may be asked to describe how your peers see you, or how you see yourself; such as describe yourself in one or two words.

- You may be asked about a person or event that impacted you.

As you can see, there are few limits to what you might be asked, but generally the interviewers are trying to get a sense of who you are, where you are headed, and how the scholarship will help you get there.

CASE STUDY: GREG ROLLETT, Social Media Specialist at the Orlando Employment Guide

So, your résumé got you through the door. Good stuff. Glad to hear it, really.

Now that you are at the door, are you prepared to answer the question that takes most people down before they start? The question that is so relatively simple, yet vague and scary, that it can single-handedly make or break your interview:

"So, Mr. (or Mrs.) Potential Employee, tell me about yourself."

Most interviewees go into the elevator pitch, 30-second sell, or whatever hot term that basically describes yourself in less time than it takes to watch a Super Bowl commercial. This is not a bad route. The problem lies within the context of how you pitch yourself.

Yes, you want to be confident, strong, and truthful. Talk about your career experiences and past employment. Most importantly and probably most overlooked is the fact that you want to sell yourself to the company. How can you help them out? What skills, background, and experience do you have that the employer can utilize to better their organization?

Here are five quick tips to answering the all-important interview question (statement), Tell Me About Yourself:

1. Be honest. They have your résumé with contact information right in front of them and they will be calling on your references. Oh, and most employers can call a bluff (it is called counter-questioning).

2. Keep it short and relevant. Find your best qualities and skills and limit it to what is important to the company that is interviewing you. There is no need to talk about the process of TV repair when interviewing for a marketing position. Think elevator pitch.

3. Practice. Do not go into the interview blind. More often than not, you have some time between the contact and the first meeting. Practice in front of a mirror, with a friend, or even a family member. (I am sure they want you to succeed and stop mooching out of their fridge.)

4. Research. When talking about yourself, blend in the company's information to show that you have done your part in the research. The internet poses as a great resource for company information.

5. Eye contact. This keeps both you and the interviewer honest and shows that you want his attention and that he in turn keeps attention to your most important details.

I hope this sheds some light into the all-important first step once you have polished your résumé enough to get in the door. Remember, an interview is your chance to really sell yourself both visually and verbally. Keep the focus on the company and be confident in yourself and your skill set, and you will be collecting a nice paycheck in no time.

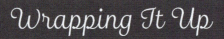

Wrapping It Up

Finding a scholarship is only half the battle. Once you find it, you may still have a long road ahead of you to get scholarship funds. You might have to fill out a lengthy application, write a personal statement, write a several-page essay, or make it through an interview with a scholarship committee. You will have to apply and apply, and you will not win every one that you apply for, but do not give up. While it all seems daunting, stressful, and time-consuming, if you break down your scholarship requirements into steps and concentrate on one thing at a time, it is not so bad. Getting free money takes time and effort, but in the end, you will be glad you went through the process, especially when you are finished with college and looking at a stack of student loans to pay.

Chapter 9

Avoiding Trouble

hen it comes to college funding, sometimes it is easy to lose sight of your goal: "Get your degree while going into the least amount of debt." You may try to fool yourself into thinking that you can pay the money back someday, or that there is no reason to worry about the money now when you have school to think about, or that you will be making so much money when you graduate, it will be easy to pay back your loans. All of this thinking is wrong. You need to think about paying money back the day you borrow it. You need to think about whether or not the payments will be so steep that you will not be able to afford rent (yes, it does happen!). You need to be responsible about your borrowing, and make sure you are aware of all of your loan terms and agreements. Keep in mind that you may not make a whole lot of money after you graduate from college. Most careers do not start you out at the top of the pay scale. You still have to work your way up. Hefty paychecks could take years of working in your career to arrive, if they ever come at all.

According to "The Project on Student Debt: An Initiative of the Institute for College Access & Success," students are going into more and more debt, averaging $28,950 in 2014, yet their salaries are not keeping up:

- There was a little more than a 58 percent increase in average student loan debt of graduating seniors between 2004 and 2014 at campuses reporting data for these years. In comparison, starting salary offers for graduating seniors rose roughly 3-4 percent in the same period.

- The average debt of the class of 2014 reported by institutions — $28,950 — is likely about $1,500 lower than the actual average, due to the limited number of campuses reporting, and deficiencies in the information available to college officials. This means that actual student debt levels are now roughly $30,400.

If you are wondering what your occupation pays, the U.S. Department of Labor Bureau of Labor Statistics offers wages that are defined by occupation and area. Although the site does not include starting salaries, it does give you a sense of what you will earn in your occupation. You can find out more at: www.bls.gov.

The Credit Card Trap

Those little plastic cards look so innocent, but they can sure get you in a lot of trouble. It is easy to forget that all that credit card spending has to be paid back with interest. And interest adds up fast! You could wind up paying twice as much for your purchase if you have a credit card with high interest that you do not pay off every month. Plus, add in late fees, overdraft fees, and you could pay three times as much for the item as it cost in the first place. Let us take a look at the credit card trap in greater detail.

College students are not the only ones who use credit cards a little too much. Most of America uses them on a regular basis, but it often ends up costing them more than they ever expected.

According to CardTrak — the nation's most established and most trusted credit card advisory service for consumers, credit card debt is indeed high:

PORT CHARLOTTE, FL (May 31, 2007) According to a survey released by CardTrak.com, the median amount of credit card debt carried by Americans is about $6,600 while the mean (or average) credit card debt load is nearly $9,900. According to Tim Chen, of NerdWallet, Inc., in 2015 average credit card debt was $16,140.

Of cardholders carrying debt, more than 64 percent had balances under $10,000. However, an astonishing 13 percent of the same group said they carry total credit card balances in excess of $25,000.

Why does a credit card wind up costing you so much more than if you would have made your purchase in cash?

- Some credit cards you have to pay to get in the first place — the fees can be anywhere from $25 to $100 or more. Plus, the credit card company charges that same fee year after year just so you can use the card.

- Some interest rates reach even higher than 22 percent. You may find low-rate cards, but often the low rate is an introductory rate, so it is short-lived.

- Penalty interest rates are typically 30 percent, up to as much as 40 percent.

- Late fees are often $39 a month. And you do not have 30 days to get your payment in on time.

- Overdraft fees are typically $35. Are you wondering why you are allowed to go over your limit? The credit card companies make money off you doing so.

- Credit card companies can increase your interest rate if you are late with your payments. All of a sudden your interest rate will jump, and if you do not pay close attention, you might not even notice that it did. You should check your statement every month to see if the rate increased. If so, find a new card!

Those are many fees that could really cost you if you do not stay on top of paying your bill on time, stay within your limit, and shop around for a low-interest card. Credit card companies stay in business by charging users these hefty fees.

So what do you do if you have racked up credit cards?

- **Don't start using them in the first place.** You are probably spending way more than you need to. When you use a credit card, you are paying entirely too much for your purchase in the long run once you add up the interest and potential fees.

- **Try to pay off the entire amount every month.** This will also stop the interest fees.

- **If you have to have one, have as few as possible.** Most of us do need one to make purchases on the internet, or to place a purchase on hold, but one or two should suffice.

- **Pay more than the minimum payment.** If you cannot pay the entire amount, pay more than the minimum payment. You will save on interest in the long run.

- **Do not be late with your payments.** Credit card companies often do not give you a full 30 days to make you payment. As soon as you get the bill, check the payment due date. Make sure you mail in the payment seven-10 days ahead of the due date, so it arrives in time. Better yet, you may want to make your payment online. Paying late causes interest rates to increase in great amounts.

- **Ask for help from your credit card company.** If you owe a lot of money on credit cards and cannot seem to make even your minimum payments, try to ask your credit card company for help. They may work with you and give you a lower interest rate, or reduce your payment. You can also request that the due date be changed if it is hard to pay at the time of month that you receive your bill. For instance, if your payment due date is the 5th of the month, you can ask that it be changed to the 15th of the month if that is easier for you.

- **Try transferring your balance to a lower-interest credit card.** Some cards offer low rates, even 6-7 percent, for a certain amount of time, sometimes for six months or for an entire year. When you receive these, just make sure that you look for another offer when the end of that time is nearing with another company, and if you make your payments on time, you can keep doing this until the loan is paid off or until one of the company's offer you a fixed low rate. Just remember, 'new' charges to this may carry heavier interest rates. And many of these offers will be rescinded if you have late payments, so make sure your payments are on time and that you keep track of when the offer ends.

- **See about home equity.** If you have home equity, it sometimes makes sense to take out a loan to pay off the credit card debt. Your interest will be less, and you can deduct the interest paid on your taxes. Check with your tax adviser for details.

- **Get debt counseling.** You might also seek help for debt through American Consumer Credit Counseling. According to their website, they are "a non-profit (501)(c)(3) organization, offering confidential credit counseling and financial education to consumers nationwide. ACCC is dedicated to helping people regain control of their finances and plan for a debt-free future." The service can assist you with everything, including lowering your monthly payment, reducing finance charges, and reducing or eliminating late fees and overdraft fees.

American Consumer Credit Counseling (ACCC)

800-769-3571

Client Service Department: ext. 500

Counseling Center: ext. 506

www.consumercredit.com

Loan Consolidation Pitfalls

While loan consolidation sounds like a great idea because you lower your payments and interest, it has its drawbacks. First, let us examine why loan consolidation is sometimes the right choice before we get into the pitfalls of consolidating your loan.

As mentioned, you typically get a lower interest rate on a consolidation loan than you do with your credit card debt. Consider that credit cards range from 13-30 percent, unless you are able to secure a lower-interest card. The minimum monthly payment is about four percent, although each credit card differs. Consolidation may make sense if you can lower the interest rate.

Chapter 5 presented home equity alternatives, which you may want to consider for loan consolidation. Check with a financial adviser before making any decisions about taking out a home equity loan or line of credit, as home equity loans and lines have drawbacks as well.

Let us take a look at a few of the benefits of loan consolidation:

- You lower your interest rate and payments.
- You can lock into a fixed lower interest rate.
- You only make one payment instead of making several to different credit card companies.
- It is easier to keep track of having just one loan, so you are less likely to be late with a payment.

- You will have a better chance of keeping on top of your payments and avoiding default on your loan.

If you have only student loans that you owe, you might think about consolidating them with a FFEL loan.

According to the U.S. Department of Education:

"A FFEL Consolidation Loan is designed to help student and parent borrowers consolidate several types of federal student loans with various repayment schedules into one loan. With a FFEL Consolidation Loan, you will make only one payment a month. Under this program, your consolidation loan will be made by a commercial lender, credit bureaus will be notified that your account has a zero balance, and you will sign a new promissory note that will establish a new interest rate and repayment schedule. To receive a FFEL Consolidation Loan, you must be in repayment on your defaulted loan (that is, three voluntary, on-time, full monthly payments). Depending on the balance due, the repayment period may extend up to 30 years. If you owe no other delinquent or defaulted debts to the United States, you will again be eligible for other federal funds, including FHA loans, VA loans, and Title IV student financial aid funds."

For more information, and to apply online for loan consolidation, visit: **www.loanconsolidation.ed.gov**.

For a complete list of the federal student loans that can be consolidated, contact:

- The Direct Loan Origination Center's Consolidation Department, if you are applying for a Direct Consolidation Loan. You can reach them by calling 800-557-7392.

TTY users may call 800-557-7395.

Or visit **www.loanconsolidation.ed.gov**.

- A participating FFEL lender, if you are applying for a FFEL Consolidation Loan. If you do not know who your FFEL lender is, call 800-433-3243 for assistance.

But before you rush out to consolidate your debt, you need to look at the whole picture, including the drawbacks.

- Debt consolidation can stretch out your loan terms, and even if you are paying less interest, you may pay more in the long run by stretching out the terms.

- Your interest rate or ability to get a loan may depend on how good your credit is. Most lenders are not going to give you an unsecured loan or will give you a less-than-stellar interest rate if your credit score is not excellent.

- You need to be careful about which loans you consolidate. There is no sense in consolidating lower interest loans, like student loans, with higher interest loans. Also, some of the loan forgiveness programs will not pay back the portion of the loan that they allow, if it is consolidated.

Additionally, there are unscrupulous lenders out there who are very eager to consolidate your loan, hoping that you will not read the fine print. These lenders charge enormous fees for initiating the loan, ridiculous late fees, and early loan payoff fees, so you have to be very careful about whom you borrow the money from in the first place. It is best to start looking for loan consolidation with your bank and see what they can offer you. Also ask your school's financial aid office if they know of a good private source for loan consolidation. Even if you do not wind up taking out your loan with your bank or with a lender that your school has recommended, you will have a basic starting point to shop around for other loan consolidations. But be on the alert and play it safe.

Some questions to ask about loan consolidation:

- What is the interest rate?
- Is it fixed or variable? If it is variable, how high can it go?
- What is the total amount of all of the loan fees?
- What are those fees for?
- How much are the payments?
- When do the payments start?
- Are there discounts available for making payments online or automatic payment withdrawals?
- Can payments be deferred or reduced? If so, what are the circumstances for doing so? How do you make a request for that?
- Is there a penalty for paying off the loan early? How much is it?

Before making a decision about your student loan, you should speak with a financial adviser.

Scholarship and Aid Scams

In Chapter 7, we touched on the topic of scholarship scams. But since it is such an enormous and expensive issue for consumers, it is worthwhile to spend some time going over possible scams in more detail.

There are plenty of ways to scam people, and scholarships, grants, and loan companies are no exception in looking for a way to bilk you out of your money or personal information.

Here are a few things to keep in mind when applying for any type of college funding or loans.

- **Do not give money away to get money.** You should not have to pay someone to find you free money. It is not free money if you have to pay someone to get it for you. Besides, you can do your own research for finding scholarships, grants, and loans for free.

- **There are no guarantees.** No one can guarantee that you will receive a grant, loan, or scholarship.

- **Be careful about giving out your identity and personal information.** Unless you are working with a reputable source such as **www.fafsa.ed.gov**, be leery of giving out your personal information, such as your social security number or bank and credit card information. Identity theft occurs often.

- **Watch out for tactics.** "Hurry" or "rush" are scare tactics to try to get you to cave in and act now. Do not trust anyone who uses these measures.

- **Read all documents carefully.** Do not forget to read the fine print. That is where the tricks are often buried.

- **Beware of the letters that get sent out to the students inviting them (and their parents) to a 'free' meeting, with promises of hundreds of scholarships and college admissions assistance.** Most of these rent a reputable room in a nice hotel or a public library and have this motivational meeting, afterwards making individual appointments — appointments where they try to talk you into writing them a large check for doing free scholarship searches that you can do yourself. Remember, once again, NO ONE can guarantee you a scholarship.

- **Make sure that you are dealing with a legitimate business.** If you have doubts, do research. Call the Better Business Bureau. Listen to your hunches. If it sounds too good to be true, it probably is.

To contact the Better Business Bureau:

> The Council of Better Business Bureaus
> 4200 Wilson Blvd, Suite 800
> Arlington, VA 22203-1838
> **www.bbb.org**

For more information on what to watch out for with scams, visit the FTC at **www.ftc.gov/scholarshipscams**.

Finaid.com offers helpful information about scholarship scams and what to watch out for at **www.finaid.org/scholarships/scams.phtml**.

Report fraud

A company charging for financial aid advice is not committing fraud unless it does not deliver what it promises. For more information about financial aid fraud or to report fraud, call the Federal Trade Commission toll free at 877-FTC-HELP or 877-382-4357, or go to **www.ftc.gov/scholarshipscams**.

Report identity theft

If you suspect that your student information has been stolen, it is important to act quickly. These offices will help you determine what steps to take depending on your situation:

> U.S. Department of Education
> Office of Inspector General Hotline
> 800-MIS-USED (1-800-647-8733)
> Federal Trade Commission
> 877-IDTHEFT (1-877-438-4338)

Scholarship Search Scams

Scholarship search scams are a category of scams. They make you pay to have them conduct searches of scholarships that you can conduct for free, and the price can be high.

According to the FTC, "scam artists guarantee 'free money for college' in campus newspapers, flyers, post cards, official looking invitations to a meeting, and on the internet. They charge from $100 to over $1,000 for their services. According to the FTC, however, students who rely on a fraudulent search service instead of doing their own homework when applying for scholarships or grants will face the upcoming school year bills with nothing for the effort but a hard-earned lesson."

Charging for these services is not illegal, but all they are doing is providing you with information that you can obtain for free from reputable sources. No scholarship search company is privy to information that you cannot find out on your own for free, such as at www.fastweb.com. Check the appendix for more resources.

What to watch out for with scholarship search scams:

- **Secret scholarships:** As mentioned above, there are never any scholarships that are secret or have secret information. Anyone taking some time and effort to find out about scholarships may do so.

- **Guarantees:** A scholarship search company cannot guarantee that you will get a scholarship even if they find one for you. No one can guarantee you free money.

- **Forcing you to make purchases:** You should not have to make a purchase to have a shot at winning a scholarship. Neither should you be subject to a plethora of pop-up windows and banners trying to entice you to spend your money.

- **Fake scholarships:** Some scholarships themselves are not even legitimate. They are pretending to be scholarships in the effort to bilk you for money or personal information and try to charge you fees to apply.

Remember to keep your personal information tightly held. Do not give out your social security number, your banking information, your PIN number, or any other information to any source that is not verified as a legitimate business.

Keep in mind that a legitimate scholarship service will not have a website with calls to action such as "Hurry!" or "Act now!" These are just pressure tactics trying to entice you to spend your money or offer your personal information before you have had time to check out the background of who is offering you information.

If you are dealing with a company that you suspect is scamming you, document everything. Get it all in writing, and report the company as soon as possible.

Dropping Courses

Sometimes whether you want to or not, you are faced with having to drop a class. You got too busy with work and/or other classes, or perhaps you are feeling burned out and you want a break. Or you decide that you hate the class that you enrolled in, took too heavy of a workload, or that the class is just too difficult for you at this time. There are many reasons why students drop classes. Dropping a class may be your best bet in some situations, if you do not think you could pass the class or you changed your mind on your course of study, provided that is it is early in the semester, and you can still get a refund.

It is always in your best interest to know when the last drop/add day for the semester is, or you could wind up with an F or a W (withdrawal). Even if you can get a refund, you may still be at a loss by dropping a class.

Some schools may only give you a partial refund for dropping a class, unless it is in the first week or so. But even then, you may still be stuck with losing money on school fees, books, and other expenses that you invested for the class.

Something else to consider before you fill out that drop slip is that by dropping a class, you may be holding down fewer credits than are allowed in order to receive funding, insurance, or other benefits. For instance, your health insurance or your car insurance may be offering you special rates if you are a full-time student. Drop a class or two and you might lose out on your full-time student discounts, so you need to find out about these things before dropping.

You also need to find out if your grants, loans, or scholarships require that you maintain a certain number of credits per semester. You could potentially lose that money if you drop a class. If you plan to drop a class, you need to find out the minimum amount of classes that you must carry. Does being a full-time student mean that you have to carry 12 credits a semester or 15 credits? How does dropping a class affect that?

Also consider your student housing. Does it require that you hold down a certain number of credits each semester? You do not want to get kicked out of your dorm room for dropping a class.

When thinking about dropping a class, you should also consider graduation. Is losing this class going to throw off your graduation date? Is it a required class, meaning you will have to take it and get it over with at some point? Is it a prerequisite for other courses so that dropping it is going to mess up your next few semesters' schedule?

Before you drop a class, find out what financial considerations you should think about, including loans, grants, scholarships, and your housing. Also find out the feasibility in terms of how this will affect your graduation plans.

If you are having trouble with a class, you could speak with your professor about how to make the class go more smoothly. Perhaps you can get a pass/fail grade instead of a letter grade, or ask about an incomplete. You could speak with your adviser and find out about tutoring. Some schools offer help with tutoring. You could buckle down and just finish the class. You have some choices, and you may find that the best one may be sticking it out and finishing the class.

Dropping Out

It is unfortunate but true that many college students do not finish their degrees.

According to Fastweb.com, "Almost 60 percent of those attending public universities do not complete their degrees within five years — and more than 70 percent of U.S. students earning four-year degrees attend public universities."

Some students cannot handle the academic rigors. Some realize that they cannot afford college. Others wind up in life-changing situations that make college infeasible. No matter what obstacles you come across, though, it is a good idea to try to finish. There are also many different certificate programs that you can receive from community or vocational colleges. Not everyone is made for going to college for a bachelor's degree or higher. With a certificate or a one- to three-year program, many jobs, like registered nurse, massage therapist, radiographer assistant, vet assistant, dental assistant or hygienist, certified welder, police officer, fire fighter, physical therapist assistant, auto mechanic, and countless other careers, will earn you much more than just going to work without any college at all.

Generally, those who earn degrees make more than those without them. Plus, if you drop out of school, you may have to pay money that was given to you as a scholarship or grant. (Check your funding source for details.) And you will begin paying your student loans much sooner.

When you think about the cost of dropping out of school, you might want to consider trying to find a way to work on your degree, even if it means only taking a few classes at a time over a longer time period.

You could look into night school, online schools, or extension classes. You can find plenty of accredited degrees from many schools that offer these alternative means of getting your education. Even at the school you are attending now, you may be able to take some of your classes online or take them during the evening to free up time for a part-time job. Or you may be able to take some of your classes through extension which is generally quite a bit cheaper than through the regular school program. For instance, at Harvard you can enroll in an extension class that ranges from $1,350 to $2,400 for four-credit courses, whereas you would pay about $5,000 per regular course. But Harvard, as in many other private schools, does not believe in loans. So if you have financial need, you could actually graduate without any loans, but if you fall in the middle class range, you will be expected to come up with more money and still may have to resort to loans or a less expensive school.

If you are having money troubles, there are things you can do to alleviate the pressure on your bank account. Have you applied for all the possible funding that you can receive for college? Have you cut your discretionary expenses? Can you cut your living expenses by getting a roommate or moving back home? Can you get a part-time job? Chapter 10 will offer a few ways to help you cut your expenses.

Before you assume you cannot afford school, consider whether you can really afford to drop. In the long run, it may cost you quite a bit more, considering lost earning potential. For example, what if you were attending college to become a doctor but wind up dropping out? How much money do you think you might lose in a lifetime by missing out on receiving a doctor's wages year after year?

Before you drop out of school, always speak with your academic adviser. He or she may have some good insights or ideas that can help you figure out a way to make staying in school work.

Wrapping It Up

Just as important to finding great deals and free money for college is staying on top of the money you have and avoiding getting scammed. Keep in mind that if something sounds a little fishy, it probably is. If it sounds too good to be true, it probably is. Keep your eyes open and your wallet and personal information close to you. If you suspect a scam, document everything and make sure you report the scam to officials.

If you are thinking about dropping a class or dropping out of school, keep in mind what you may run into financially. Dropping a class may cost you your scholarship, your housing, or even your insurance. Dropping out of school can cost you a lifetime of lost earnings. Think hard before making decisions about your school. Speak with your adviser about the implications of your school decisions. He or she may have the right advice to help you make the right decision.

Chapter 10

Living Cheap

hroughout this book we have focused on how to bring more money into your pockets by applying for grants, scholarships, loans, and more. During this chapter, we will concentrate on ways that you can cut back on your expenses, including factors like where you live, how you can cut medical expenses, and where you can find deals on books and supplies. Even if you get a great deal of money from scholarships and grants, it is still a good idea to cut your expenses down to a minimum. You would be surprised how fast money goes out the door, even with the free money helping. And if you think you can cover all the extras with the aid of student loans, remember that keeping your student loans down to a minimum is your best bet. We will explore the many ways you can save on your living expenses and keep the cost of going to school as inexpensive as it can be.

Choosing Where to Live

Where you decide to go to school may make your decision for you in terms of the area that you will live. However, if you have a few schools that you are interested in attending and they cost about the same amount of money for tuition, you might want to look into the cost of living at the college. If you are staying in a dorm, how much does it cost? What does it include? If you are staying in student housing, what is the rent? If the school is located in a big city, you might have big city expenses that you might not incur in a smaller town. Plus, the food and gas may be higher as well. There are different websites that can help you find what the cost of living is in the town you are considering. For instance, Data-

Masters offers surveys where you can find out about the cost of living, along with your expected salary for your field (**www.datamasters.com**).

Another website that provides you with a list of cities or towns that might best fit you is "Find Your Spot." The site has you fill out a short survey of what you want and do not want in a city or town and you are given a few ideas of places that would suit you. This makes some sense to look into while going to college and upon graduation (**www.findyourspot.com**).

Choosing which city might fit your budget is only part of the equation. If you have already decided on a certain school and city you have choices to make about where you are living. You can choose to live on campus or off. You can choose to have roommates or live alone. You can choose to live within driving distance or walking distance, or you can choose to live on a bus route. You can choose to be in the middle of the action or live in a quieter place. If you are attending school online, you can choose to live anywhere. Where you decide to live is based on your budget, your lifestyle, your personality, and what is important to you.

When trying to make a decision about where to live, you might want to think about the positives and negatives for each situation. For instance, if you are contemplating having a roommate, you may think about the extra money you will save on rent and the possibility of having company or friendship. The negatives might be that you have to share a space with a person who may be sloppy, loud, or parties too much — especially when you are trying to study. If you are thinking about a dorm room, you may enjoy all the socializing that comes along with it, but the dorm may have certain rules that you have to abide by, such as curfews. Think about the positives and the negatives for each choice you make, and hopefully you will be able to make the right decision for where to live during college. It really depends on what is right for you.

Dorms are also often more expensive than college apartments, which are also rented to college students, but by private citizens. Dorms usually have meal plans that can be costly, and some only cover nine or 15 meals weekly. You need to find out what happens if you do not use all of your meals for one week. Do they roll over to another week? Another huge benefit to an apartment is that you usually have the bedroom to yourself and either have the bathroom too or only have to share it with one other person (versus an entire floor at a dorm).

CASE STUDY: SUSAN JOHNSTON, Freelance Writer

Cheap Dorm Room Decorating Ideas and Tips

Your dorm room will be a home away from home, so it should be a place where you can study effectively and provide safe sanctuary from outside stress.

Here are a few suggestions for making it comfortable and stylish:

The Basics of Bedding

The bed often doubles as a coffee table, couch, or study area, so it is key to choose a comforter that reflects your style and will not immediately show the dirt. A comforter helps determine the color scheme for the rest of the room, so choose one you like. Reversible, solid-colored comforters are a good choice, because they offer twice as many design options.

Think Storage

Space is tight in most dorms, so maximizing storage is a must. Try raising the bed with cement blocks or RackRisers to make space under the bed. You can also stack plastic crates in your closet, under your bed, or next to your desk. An alternative to plastic crates is a wire storage system, which lets you assemble your own crates and dismantle or reorganize them later. Or use decorative hat boxes in varying sizes. Buy closet organizers for shoes, skirts, accessories, or makeup. Also invest in some cheap plastic hooks, and just stick them to your closet door to hold a bathrobe or jacket. Tables can do double-duty for TVs and computers.

The Wall Is Your Canvas

Always check your school's rules before painting, punching holes, or even using tape on the walls. Some colleges have a poster sale at the beginning of the year where you can snag some highly unusual and inexpensive finds. Poster adhesive, found at decorating stores, can be safely used. Unleash your inner artist and draw a new mural or work of art once a month or whenever you feel inspired by using colored chalk, or butcher paper and colored pencils. Frames are essential for holding photos of home or new friends. French memo boards can hold a whole bunch of pictures, ticket stubs, or magazine cutouts. A laundry line is a great alternative for you to string up pictures or ticket stubs on the wall or across the room. Magnets are useful and decorative on any metal surface. Dry erase boards are handy for communicating with friends and roommates and keeping track of your busy schedule.

Other Thoughts

Sheer fabric draped across the window or over a bed creates a soft, romantic look. If you have an open closet, put up a colorful shower curtain to individualize your space or hide dirty laundry. A desk lamp for late-night studying is a necessity, but adding mini-lights across the room can create a more personal atmosphere. White lights will complement any décor, or choose colored lights in funky shapes like stars, cactuses, or hearts.

To Drive or Not to Drive

If you want to help the environment, we should all be walking or riding bikes. While that is not totally possible, it is something to consider doing when you can. Besides offering a clean-air alternative, bike riding keeps you in shape and keeps your stress level lower. If you do not have a bike, you can usually find a good deal on a new one at a sporting goods store. Otherwise, keep your eyes open for a good used one in the want ads, online at sites like **www.craigslist.com,** or at garage sales. You may just find a great bike that is hardly used.

Many students also use skateboards as a quick way to get around on campus, especially larger ones, but that does require a few more skills than bike riding, and they are not road friendly. You may be living in a location where it is not possible to bike. Perhaps it is too cold or you live to far from school, or maybe you are taking night classes, and it is unsafe to walk or bike. Can you consider the bus? Buses are also better for the environment, and they are a lot cheaper for you to use for transportation — much more than driving a car or even a scooter. Some cities offer bus passes for the month where you pay a flat fee for unlimited rides. For instance, in Los Angeles, monthly LADOT passes start at $57 per month. That is a whole lot less than it costs to drive a car, especially once you consider gas, maintenance, and insurance. Check with your city for details on bus passes.

If you are living in a city such as Chicago, New York, or San Francisco, you can easily get around without a car. You have options such as trains, cabs, and buses that are a cheaper alternative than owning a car.

If you cannot walk, ride a bike, or take the bus, you can save money when using your car by taking several measures:

- **Carpool.** Find fellow students that need rides, and get them to chip in for gas. If you do not know anyone that wants to carpool, you can post a notice on a school bulletin board, in the school newspaper, or on social media.

- **Use a gas credit card.** Some gas credit cards give you money back for purchases. You have to purchase gas anyway, so you might as well get a rebate.

- **Drive a fuel-efficient car.** If you have not bought a car yet, make sure you purchase one that gets good gas mileage. Or better yet, buy a hybrid.

  For better fuel efficiency:

  - Keep your tires well-inflated.
  - Change your air filter frequently.
  - Keep your car tuned up.
  - Avoid long idles if you can.
  - Use the air conditioning less.
  - Do not top off your gas.

- **Cut out unnecessary trips.** Think about where you are driving and try to do all your errands while on the trip without backtracking. Figure out the shortest way to get from point A to point B when driving anywhere. Purchasing a GPS may be a good idea.

- **Walk some, and drive some.** Perhaps you cannot get away from owning a car, but you can try to walk or bike to your location sometimes. The gas you can save will really add up.

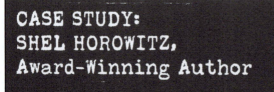

CASE STUDY:
SHEL HOROWITZ,
Award-Winning Author

What could be better for the frugal college student than... the humble bicycle?

The bike is one of the most empowering technologies ever invented: a combination weight-loss, fitness, recreation, transportation, and exploration device. It allows you to spend time with loved ones or by yourself, having FUN! Whether you prefer to fly down a hillside at top speed or cruise leisurely through a beautiful park, the bike offers you a chance to do it.

Consider this:

- A bicycle costs almost nothing to operate, and its manufacturing impact is a lot lighter on the earth than a car, motorbike, or moped.

- In crowded urban areas, bikes are often faster than cars on trips up to about 5 miles (roughly 9 km if my math is right), and the majority of car trips are less than that.

- Rural areas with poor public transit are often delightful places to ride: hardly any traffic, clean air, open scenery.

- Even people with certain disabilities can often enjoy a bike ride — on a hand-powered recumbent model, for instance.

- There's nothing as good as a bike for getting from one end of campus to the other quickly and without hassle.

- Bike paths, bicycle parking, bike racks on public buses, showers, and other amenities have been installed in many areas — and if your area is behind the times, start asking for what you want!

I started commuting by bicycle as a sophomore in high school, in New York City. My trip was three miles of flat terrain. But when we moved a year later, my ride was 5-1/2 miles uphill. On my three-speed, I still routinely beat the bus, which took a convoluted route.

Later, when I worked in Manhattan, I would bike several miles to a better subway station with a more direct route to work. Even after moving to New England, I still used my bike constantly to get around town. Now, unfortunately, we are in a steep, curvy area along a state highway, and it is much harder. But I still bike to the post office sometimes, or strap the bikes to the car, drive a few miles, and ride along the bike path. Some bus companies are even installing bike racks now. The ability to combine bikes with other modes of transportation provides incredible flexibility.

So, what are you waiting for? Get that old bike out of the garage, pump up the tires, and go for it!

Shel Horowitz is the owner of **www.frugalfun.com** *and the author of The Penny-Pinching Hedonist: How to Live Like Royalty with a Peasant's Pocketbook — a 280-page book on how to have fun cheaply — as well as several business books on frugal and ethical marketing.*

Doing Without

Like most Americans, you are probably caught up in consumerism. You are buying things you do not need, or even want, because you feel like you have to or it is on sale. Thanks to the bombardment of advertising, many of us are caught in the consumerism trap. We end up spending way too much money, more than we make, and more than we need to. How can you stop?

Start by keeping track of your expenses and preparing a budget. Following a budget helps limit your extra spending. Buy a small notebook, and start keeping track of where your money is going. You can always use budgeting software, but a notebook is cheaper and works just as well. After a week or so, take a look. You will be surprised to see where the money is going. Some of it is going to fixed expenses, such as rent, gas, insurance, and other expenses that really do not change and are necessary. Other money is going out to discretionary expenses. Those are expenses that are not set every month. It is where you can really look at cutting back on spending first. But you can always try to lower your fixed expenses by moving to a less expensive apartment, getting cheaper insurance, or even selling your car.

Once you see where the money is going, you can look at ways to reduce spending. For instance, if you are eating out every single day for every meal at an average price of $8 per meal, that's $720 per month for food. Surely, you do not need to spend that much on food every month. Buy some groceries, and make some meals at home, like sandwiches. Sandwiches are just as quick and easy as fast food and probably a whole better for your health.

You should also take a look at your impulse buying. Stores are set up to offer these impulse purchases right by the register, such as candy bars and magazines, so you ponder buying them while waiting in line. Cut back on those impulses. Even if you are only spending one dollar here and there, those add up pretty quickly.

Another place to curtail your finances may be with your entertainment. While it may be fun to go out with your friends, why not try inviting them to your house instead of meeting them at a local pub? If you enjoy going to the movies, try renting movies at least some of the time instead. Netflix is much less expensive than going to the movies. You do not have to completely change your lifestyle to cut back on spending, but you can alter it some and save money in the process.

When it comes to clothing, try thrift stores or consignment stores. You can usually find what you need for just a few dollars, and you can usually take your old clothes there on consignment to make a little money at the same time.

There are a multitude of great websites out there that offer innovative ideas for living on less. You should check them out for ideas on how to incorporate some of this into your life — at least until you finish school.

A few good frugal sites:

- **www.thefrugallife.com** — Contains information on how to live frugally with what you have.
- **www.livingonadime.com** — Offers newsletters and articles with money-saving tips.
- **www.zenhabits.net** — Offers a forum to help you save on money by cutting back on expenses through 50 Tips for Frugal Living.

You could also check for free stuff at **www.freecycle.org**. According to Freecycle, "Our mission is to build a worldwide gifting movement that reduces waste, saves precious resources, and eases the burden on our landfills while enabling our members to benefit from the strength of a larger community."

Eating Right

Even if you are a poor college student, it is important to eat healthy. Eating healthy will give you more energy, make you feel better and stronger, improve your memory for classes, lower your risk of disease, and keep you living longer. Even if you do not have lots of money, you can still eat healthy.

If you are looking for best bargains at the grocery store, try shopping in the perimeters. The middle aisles are packed full of prepackaged and expensive foods. The healthiest food is found in the outside aisles. Bring along a list of things to buy when you go to the grocery store. You will cut back on impulse purchases, which will leave more money to buy healthy foods. If you buy bulk items and split them with a friend or roommate, that will help shave costs, too. Also, if you have a food co-op available, you might want to try shopping there before the grocery store. Co-ops are customer-owned business that offer high-quality, fresh, locally grown foods to their members — all at a great value.

You can find local farmers markets by visiting:

- **www.farmersmarket.com**
- **https://www.ams.usda.gov/services/local-regional**

Do not forget farmers' markets and roadside fruit and vegetable stands. They are often loaded with great deals on local foods. Many veggies can be packed in your backpack if you get the munchies, such as mini-carrots and cut celery. Frozen veggies also work, as they stay fresh in the freezer and do not go to waste.

Drink plenty of water. If you are looking for the cheapest drink available, look no further than your kitchen faucet. Some city water actually tastes just fine, so even if you drink some bottled water, you can still tap into the tap and save money. Remember that drinking eight glasses of water every day is good for your digestive tract and keeps you hydrated and refreshed.

You do not need meat every meal. Cheap sources of protein can be found in beans, eggs, and whey powders that you can use for shakes. Check at your local health food store or even a large supermarket for a container of whey powder.

For breads, opt for whole-grain breads and cereals. They may cost a little more, but they are much better for you. You can also find day-old bread stores where the bread still tastes good and is much cheaper.

A few more tips about saving money on food:

- **Do not forget about generic and store-brand items.** The taste is often just as good or better than the name brand, and they are generally quite a bit cheaper.

- **Plan your meals, and write down what you need.** That way when you head to the grocery store, you are buying the items you need (not extras) and not forgetting anything — plus, it saves a trip back to the grocery store and gas money.

- **Try to eat less.** Yes, you can save money by cutting back on eating, especially if you are snacking out of boredom or frustration. You not only save money, but you stay in better shape.

- **Do not eat junk food.** It is not good for you, and it is more expensive.

- **Eat out less often.** It is definitely more expensive than eating at home, especially when you add in a tip and gas for getting there.

- **If you can cut coupons, do so.** Only cut out the ones that offer you deals on food you will buy. There is no sense in purchasing items that are on sale, only to let them rot in your cupboard.

Healthy snack ideas

- Water. You may not really be hungry but instead just thirsty. Try water first.
- A can of soup fills you up. Make sure it is low in sodium.
- Microwaveable oatmeal. You can enjoy it in many different flavors.
- Dried fruits such as raisins, apricots, or cranberries.
- Crackers or pretzels. Opt for whole grain or whole wheat.
- Nuts and trail mix. You can always make your own trail mix. It is cheaper to make a batch, and you can add in just what you want.
- Granola bars.
- Fresh fruits or veggies. Slice up a few for the week.

CASE STUDY: CHARLI MILLS, Food Writer

Organizing a Pantry to Save Time and Money

We live in an era of mega-supermarkets, modern appliances, and fast food. Everything is designed to be quick, quick, quick. Yet, to the college student living on a shoe string, convenience is expensive.

Organizing a pantry can help you save time, money, and gas. When I was a college student, I had three young children and a household to manage. Money was tight. When my oldest daughter went to college, she remembered how we cooked from scratch and organized our shopping. This early influence helped her save money while in college.

A pantry is a place to store food that does not require refrigeration. It can be any kind of storage space. You want to store inexpensive staples in your pantry to extend your food budget and reduce your trips to the grocery store.

To save time, organize according to what you use. Create space for different meals. You can post a corkboard on the inside door of your pantry area to keep track of schedules, menus, and grocery lists. Take time to create a weekly menu so you are less apt to order out or skip a meal. It will also reduce the number of visits to the store. As you run out of staples, note it on your grocery list.

Take advantage of sales, and stock up if you can. Be careful not to buy on impulse, and avoid prepackaged meals. If possible, buy in bulk. Most staples like grains, pasta, and dried fruit are available in bulk. Use jars as containers, which can be found at most secondhand stores or by reusing jam or peanut butter jars. Bulk is always less expensive than packaged counterparts.

Having a pantry requires a commitment to cooking from scratch, but it is not as difficult as it sounds. For instance, homemade soups, pasta dishes, and bread are easy enough to learn how to make. Recipes are available online, at stores, and from family members. Cooking can be a group activity with roommates or classmates pitching in and sharing the results. A large crockpot is an inexpensive investment and makes preparing food easy.

Here is an organized list for a well-stocked pantry:

Breakfast Pantry Staples	
• Granola	• Cereal
• Jam	• Oatmeal
• Cream of Wheat	• Maple syrup
• Pancake mix	

Lunch Pantry Staples	
• Canned tuna	• Peanut butter
• Bread (homemade)	• Dried fruit
• Crackers (homemade)	• Seeds (less expensive than nuts)

Dinner Pantry Staples	
• Rice	• Pasta
• Dried beans	• Canned tomatoes
• Canned vegetables	• Canned broth
• Tomato paste and sauce	• Cooking oils and vinegars

Bulk Staples & Spices	
• Flour	• Oats
• Whey	• Sugar
• Cocoa powder	• Baking Soda
• Baking powder	• Salt
• Pepper	• Garlic
• Dried onions	• Oregano
• Cumin	• Chili powder
• Parsley	• Any ethnic spices like curry

Raid your parents' pantry when you visit, and keep yours organized and in regular use. For fresh items, consider looking for local dairies or farms that will sell you milk, cheese, eggs, and even beef, chicken, or pork. Carpool to the grocery store, co-op, farmers market, or farm. Master an organized pantry, and you will succeed in living on a shoe string.

Medical Expenses

While you cannot always change the fact that you will incur medical expenses, there are ways that you can cut back on your bills.

For instance, if you are taking a prescription, it is best to always ask for the generic version, as it can be substantially cheaper than the name-brand version of the medication. Also, if you are taking an expensive medication, it makes sense to shop around for the best deal. Yes, pharmacies do charge different amounts. You can also apply for an activated

Rx discount card, which can yield savings of up to 75 percent at more than 54,000 national and regional pharmacies.

If you need to go to the doctor, find out if your school has an on-campus health center, or find a free or low-cost clinic. You can generally get basic healthcare even if you have no insurance (although many colleges require you to have it) and payment is usually on a sliding fee scale. At the U.S. Department of Health and Human Services' site, you can find an HRSA-supported health center in most cities and many rural areas. To find one in your area, visit: **http://findahealthcenter.hrsa.gov**.

According to the U.S. Department of Health and Human Services, health centers provide:

- Checkups when you are well
- Treatment when you are sick
- Complete care when you are pregnant
- Immunizations and well-child care for your children
- Dental care and prescription drugs for your family

For instance, in California, the Venice Family Clinic provides free, quality healthcare to low-income patients who lack private health insurance — including comprehensive primary healthcare, mental health services, health education and child development services, along with prescription medicines that are provided at no charge. Their website is **www.venicefamilyclinic.org**.

If you need dental care, you might try a dental school for basic cleaning and some dental care. The work at the schools is generally performed by students but is supervised by experienced dentists.

For instance, at the University of Minnesota Dental Clinics, general and specialty dental care in association with the School of Dentistry's educational programs are provided to more than 100,000 patients per year — all for a fraction of what it would cost to visit a dentist.

A few tips to save on medical bills and insurance:

- **Double-check your medical bills.** You would not believe how often your bill is wrong, and you do not want to be overpaying (this is a lifelong tip).

- **Shop around for health insurance.** Think about a high deductible or even major medical. Many of your parents' insurance companies allow you to remain on their account while you are still in school.

- **Look into different co-pays on your insurance.** The higher your co-pay, the less you pay for the monthly premium.

- **Try to negotiate for a self-pay arrangement with your doctor.** They often offer cheaper rates for self-pay.

- **Reduce co-payments.** Negotiate prices with your doctors.

Your best medicine is always to take care of your health and teeth in the first place. You will look better, feel better, and stay healthier for longer.

Here are a few tips for staying healthy:

- **Make sure you get enough sleep.** You need at least eight hours nightly, not four or five. Without enough sleep, your body cannot rest and repair itself. Plus, you will be drowsy and perform less effectively.

- **Make sure that you eat a healthy diet.** Your diet should include plenty of fruits and vegetables, whole grains, and proteins every day.

- **Take a multivitamin every day.**

- **Get your exercise.** Try to get at least 30 minutes a day.

- **Do not smoke.** It is not only bad for you, but it is an expensive habit.

- **Keep your stress level down.** While going to college can be stressful, there are ways you can reduce your stress:

  - ⇉ Breathe deeply
  - ⇉ Meditate
  - ⇉ Take long walks
  - ⇉ Do something you enjoy
  - ⇉ Enjoy the company of others
  - ⇉ Talk it over with friends
  - ⇉ Keep caffeine to a minimum

Cheap Books

According to National Public Radio, "More than a dozen states are considering laws that would restrict price increases for college textbooks. With many books now costing more than $200, college students and their families are facing huge bills on top of tuition costs."

Why? Because books are a tremendous expense for students to incur on top of all the other expenses, such as tuition, fees, and housing. Some of the instructors have actually written the textbooks, so there is that to consider as well. Plus, every year it seems there is a new edition, driving students to always have to purchase the latest copy and hence doing away with the ability to make purchases of used books. Plus, books often have CD-ROMs that are enclosed with the books, just to drive up the cost even more.

Do we need all those expensive textbooks? Probably not, now that the internet and e-books are so available. Hopefully someday some of the demand for buying textbooks for college classes will be limited or eliminated, but until then, we need to make the best of it and get the books as cheaply as possible.

There are various organizations that are working on policies to help lower the cost of textbooks, such as **www.studentpirgs.org/campaigns/ sp/make-textbooks-affordable**. According to them, there are ways you can save on textbooks.

Five ways to save on textbooks

- **Buy or rent textbooks online.** There are hundreds of sites where students can buy, sell, and even rent textbooks for a fraction of the cost. Some basics include www.amazon. com, **www.campusbooks.com**, and **www.half.ebay.com**. To find other good websites, here are some keywords to search:

"used textbooks," "[your school] bookswap," "textbook price comparison," or any ISBN.

- **Shop overseas.** Many American textbooks are available at a fraction of their cost through overseas websites. Check out foreign versions of leading American websites like **www. amazon.co.uk** or get overseas prices for Thomson Learning books by going directly to their website and clicking another country at the main page. Shipping can often take several weeks, so make sure to leave enough time. Also, foreign editions may have minor differences, so as a rule of thumb, make sure the ISBN matches.

- **Swap.** There are many ways to find used books to buy, borrow, or trade just by contacting other students:

  - ➤ **Ask around:** Ask your friends, your friends' roommates, etc. It is not hard to find someone who has taken the class before, and you will save on shipping, too.

  - ➤ **Facebook (and other social media):** Look for used book groups, and search for people who have taken the class before. Try Craigslist also.

  - ➤ **Bookswaps:** Use nonprofit student-to-student sites or your student government's website.

- **Check it out.** School libraries often stock copies of commonly used textbooks. If you get there early you might be lucky enough to check one out, but at the very least, instructors will typically put one copy on reserve at the library for everyone to access. If you cannot get a book for free, you might still save money by renting. There are several online rental programs that might have the book you need, and several colleges and communities have locally based programs.

- **Do your homework.** Ask professors if you can use an older edition or a version without any "bundled" items like CDs. To make the search easier, ask your instructor for the ISBN number, which is the unique code for each book.

Here are a few other good sites to buy and sell used textbooks:

- **www.textbookx.com**
- **www.bigwords.com**
- **www.iCollegeWeb.com**
- **www.chegg.com** (and you can rent, buy, and sell them)
- **www.half.ebay.com**

These sites offer long-term solutions for lowering the prices, as well as recent news about what is happening in the legal sector with regard to lowering the cost of textbooks.

So what is so great about buying online?

- It is fast and easy.
- You save money buying used textbooks.
- You can generally find the textbooks you need.

Keep in mind that you will also incur shipping expenses when purchasing online. Remember that you will need to save the box they came in for return if renting or if you want to sell them back.

The Cost of Going Home

If you are living close to home while attending school, making a trip back home is relatively easy. You fill up your tank, jump in your car, and head out. If you want to save on gas, find out if you can carpool with a fellow student. For others, though, the process of heading home is much more involved and costly. For many students, going home can cost hundreds of dollars in travel expenses and hundreds more in lost wages that may be involved from missing work. When signing up for any college, you need to consider how far you are away from home and how often you will need to go there as part of your expenses of going to college.

If flying is your best option, make sure you check around for the cheapest deal on airfare. However, those deals might be the biggest hassles with so many restrictions to consider. For instance, you may have many stops and layovers, the layovers may be long, you may only be able to travel on certain days at certain times, you may not be able to travel on weekends, you may have a high penalty to pay for changes, or you may not be entitled to a refund should you cancel. Whenever you book a flight, you need to read the fine print carefully.

Save money on airfare

- Remember prices are higher on the holidays and often during midsummer.
- Look at different airports in the area to see if there is a cheaper alternative to depart or arrive from.
- Check **www.expedia.com**, **www.travelzoo.com**, **www.orbitz.com**, and **www.travelocity.com** to see if you can find a less expensive rate.
- Also check on the airlines' own websites.
- You might want to talk to a travel agent that specializes in budget travel.
- Find out about red-eye flights.
- Book at least two weeks in advance for the best deals.

If you have some time, you might benefit by seeing what a train ride home costs. Find out if Amtrak goes to your area and what a train ride costs by visiting: **www.amtrak.com** or even travel on a Greyhound Bus.

If you cannot afford to go home often, you could consider staying longer when you do go. That would cut down on travel expenses.

Spring Break

Spring break has its positives. You go off and unwind with your fellow students and have a great time. You might visit a place you have not been to before, perhaps even a foreign country like Mexico or the Bahamas. You might meet life-long friends. You could have the trip of a lifetime, one that you will never forget. However, while spring break is a time to enjoy, you need to be smart, careful and responsible — for both your personal safety and your money. First off, decide if you can really afford to go on a vacation. If you have to tap into your loan money, then your answer should be a definite no. This is a luxury that can be passed by. Instead, find local free things (like the beach or a lake) to do. If you plan on going somewhere, you should consider the following before you book a trip:

- If you are booking through a tour operator, make sure that the organization is reputable and well established. To find out, contact the Student and Youth Travel Association (**www.syta.org**). They describe themselves as "a non-profit, professional trade association whose mission is to promote and support integrity and professionalism among student and youth travel service providers."

SYTA offers a "Free Travel Safety Tips" brochure on their site, which includes a section on "Questions Parents Should Ask." The brochure is available free of charge on the website or by calling the number above.

You can also contact the Better Business Bureau to find out about a tour company (**www.bbb.org**).

When traveling on spring break, or any time, keep in mind these important safety tips:

- When going out, always go in groups.
- Do not leave your food or drink unattended. Do not accept drinks from strangers. Do not leave intoxicated friends alone.
- Keep your valuables and money locked up in your hotel's safe deposit box. Do not leave your passport and other important documents in your purse or wallet.
- Always wear sunscreen. When lying by the pool or ocean, you are even more susceptible to burns because of the reflection of sunlight off of the water.

- Do not travel with illegal substances. In a foreign country, you could end up in their prison.

- Be careful and smart about any sexual interactions.

The American Medical Association offers these suggestions for how to speak with college kids before a spring break trip. You could use the advice to make your trip safer and less costly:

Top 10 Things to Discuss with Your College Student Before Spring Break

1. Talk to your college student about the health and personal physical safety dangers of excessive alcohol consumption — both by themselves and others (i.e., fighting, drunk driving, and rape).

2. Give your college student tips on how to protect themselves such as traveling in pairs, having money for taxis or public transportation, carrying medical insurance cards and condoms.

3. If your son or daughter is using a tour company to plan their trip, ask to see any promotional materials that helped your college student decide. Make sure that the company is reputable and that it is not using excessive alcohol promotion to target and influence students.

4. Ask your son or daughter to provide the names and numbers of any hotels they will be staying in, as well as cellphone numbers for themselves and their friends.

5. Talk to your son or daughter about your expectations and limits with regard to alcohol use.

6. Give them a pre-paid calling card, and establish a regular check-in time.

7. Offer to cover the cost of participating in an alternative spring break program.

8. Teach your son or daughter the signs of alcohol poisoning so that they can better protect their peers and themselves.

9. If your son or daughter is under 21, makes sure that their spring break destination has the same drinking age limitations as do U.S. locations. International locations may allow students as young as 18 to legally purchase alcohol (e.g., Cancun, Mexico).

10. Warn your college student about the dangers of drinking and dehydration.

Something you could consider doing instead of traveling for spring break is to create your own spring break without leaving. Instead of spending your hard-earned cash running off to a strange location and opening up the possibilities to get scammed, you could stay close to home and take advantage of what is in your area. For instance, you could spend your week exploring the local parks, enjoying the museums, watching movies, and spending time with your friends. By staying close to home, you will no doubt spend less money than you would traveling, and you may enjoy it just as much. Do not forget your college ID for student discounts.

CASE STUDY: JENNY PHILLIPS, Owner of TravelByJen.Com, Inc.

Whether college students are heading off to spring break or home for the holidays, they can save money on travel by using the right resources and travel agencies that they can trust. TravelByJen.Com is a nationwide agency offering domestic and international vacation and cruise packages. We specialize in discounted space and deal with all types of travel including but not limited to student travel packages and spring break packages. We work with students to find the best deals and the best rates from reputable sources, and the trip enjoyment is tenfold, while the savings can be substantial.

For instance, we had a group of four girls who wanted to go the Oasis Cancun last year — one of the most popular spring break hotels in Cancun — and a competing spring break company was offering a seven-night package for $700 per person for air and hotel (provided that all four stayed in the same room). Using a travel consolidator that does over a billion dollars in business in Cancun throughout the year, I was able to get them the same hotel, but the deal I got them was an all-inclusive stay in two rooms for $799 per person. So for $99 per person, they were able to have all their meals and drinks (alcoholic as well) included in the price. The girls each had their own bed and most importantly, two bathrooms instead of one.

While you might hear about cheaper deals elsewhere, you might not be happy with what you are getting. At TravelByJen.Com, we typically stay away from "spring break tour" companies, because they tend to have less dependable flight arrangements, more problems than usual, and below-average customer service when there are problems. Plus, they try to entice you with exclusive parties and meal deals, but the truth is that these offers are available to everyone or you can forego those options and not be restricted to when and where you eat and drink. Aside from that, their rates on average are higher than normal travel companies. Why does this happen? A spring break tour company only operates for about six weeks per year, so they typically get the lower level of flights, times, and hotel contracts versus a company that will book and operate travel all year round.

If you are looking to save money on airfare home, consider traveling a day or so earlier or later. Airfares are often higher on the weekends and lower during the week, so heading home on a Friday and coming back on Monday could be hundreds of dollars cheaper.

Contact us for your travel plans, and we will come up with some affordable options that you will not find just anywhere. After all, not only do we get exclusive inventory that hotels and airlines want to sell at deep discounts, but also, as an agency, we are not obligated to sell only particular airlines or hotels. This means that we can essentially mix and match offers to get the lowest possible rate.

Staying in School

So you have made it through the application process, received a few scholarships, gotten your student loans, figured out your housing, and are busy with your studies. But you are feeling frustrated with the workload, overwhelmed with the schedule, and just cannot figure out how to do your homework assignment. Whatever you do, do not give up and drop out. Your school probably has plenty of resources available to help you ease into school and stick it out until graduation.

If you are unhappy, you need to first figure out what it is that you are unhappy with, for instance:

- If you are having a hard time making friends, try joining a campus club, or getting a part-time job on campus, which would also put a little extra cash in your pocket.

- If you are struggling with your homework, find out if there is on-campus tutoring available. Even online schools offer tutoring, so there is a good chance you can find help.

- If it is money you are worried about, try getting a part-time job, or keep applying for scholarships and grants. Figure out ways to cut back on your expenses.

- If you do not like your roommate, see if it is possible to switch rooms.

- If you do not like your major, think about switching to another one.

You do not have to sit back and be unhappy when there are things you can do to make your school experience so much better, and it pays to stay in school.

Besides a chance to earn higher pay, there are other things to consider, such as the greater ease of attending school while you are younger and not having as many responsibilities. There is also the social aspect to consider, as people may give a college-degree person more respect, and you might have a better chance of being promoted at work if you have a college degree. So do not drop out, because there are many good reasons to stay in school.

Wrapping It Up

Even if you have received a sufficient amount of college funding for tuition and expenses, there are still other expenses that you will incur and need to be considered, such as travel and medical expenses. If you try hard enough you can cut your expenses down in all areas during your college years. Look around for the best deals every time you spend money. Think twice about whether or not you need something. Cutting expenses will lessen what you borrow on loans or credit cards. If you are considering dropping out of college, think first about why you are unhappy. There is probably a way to make your college years much happier and more productive. College is a huge commitment and a big expense, but the payoff is tremendous.

Conclusion

erhaps you are still pondering if you should proceed with, or even finish, getting your college degree. And you are trying to figure out if all the money, time, and effort pays off in a financial sense. Hopefully, it is now clear that with a college degree, you still come out way ahead. According to the latest U.S. Census Bureau's report titled "Work-Life Earnings by Field of Degree and Occupation for People with a Bachelor's Degree" (2011), those with the lowest education can expect to make less than $1 million in their lifetimes while those with a professional degree can expect to make about $4 million. On average, those who attain a bachelor's degree can expect to make around $2.4 million in his or her lifetime.

Here is a chart featured in the report (see the full report here: **www.census.gov/prod/2012pubs/acsbr11-04.pdf**) which maps out the average work-life earnings by educational attainment:

Table 1.
Synthetic Work-Life Earnings by Educational Attainment
(In dollars. For information on confidentiality protection, sampling error, nonsampling error, and definitions, see *www.census.gov/acs/www*)

Educational attainment	Synthetic work-life earnings	Margin of error[1]
None to 8th grade	936,000	7,000
9th to 12th grade	1,099,000	7,000
High school graduate	1,371,000	3,000
Some college	1,632,000	5,000
Associate's degree	1,813,000	9,000
Bachelor's degree	2,422,000	8,000
Master's degree	2,834,000	13,000
Professional degree	4,159,000	33,000
Doctorate degree	3,525,000	29,000

Note: Synthetic work-life earnings represent expected earnings over a 40-year time period for the population aged 25–64 who maintain full-time, year-round employment the entire time. Calculations are based on median annual earnings from a single point in time for eight 5-year age groups and multiplied by five.
[1] The margin of error can be interpreted roughly as providing a 90 percent probability that the interval defined by the estimate minus the margin of error and the estimate plus the margin of error (the lower and upper confidence bounds) contains the true value.
Source: U.S. Census Bureau, 2011 American Community Survey.

No matter how you present the information, it almost always pays off to earn a college degree.

But what about happiness, you wonder? Does happiness not count? Is it all about money? No, it is not all about money. In addition to potentially providing you with more wealth in your lifetime, having a college degree has been shown to add to your happiness. According to a Pew Research Center survey, "College grads are happier than those without a college degree." Moreover, the Pew Research Center also found that "College-educated adults and high-income adults marry at higher rates and divorce at lower rates than do those with less education and income. They are also less likely to have children outside of marriage."

Even with all the advantages of getting your college degree, when you are just starting your first year of college, the whole process seems so immense and hard to finish. But like everything else that is worth doing, it takes some dedication and effort.

When you think about being able to write your educational background on your résumé — B.A., M.A., Ph.D. — as well as increasing your chances of being promoted on the job, making more money than you would have if you did not finish, and being happier and perhaps healthier, all that time and effort you put into going to college will be well worth it. You will be glad you went ahead and finished your degree, no matter what the cost.

Additional Resources

*T*he following websites may be helpful in your quest to find cash for school. The websites were mentioned in the book, but here they are again for your reference. There are plenty more out there.

Colleges and Universities Information

www.co-op.edu
National Commission for Cooperative Education.

www.guidetoonlineschools.com
An education directory specializing in online degrees, online schools, and distance learning.

www.kellyservices.us
Kelly Services provides staffing services and employment opportunities in all states across the U.S.

www.ncsu.edu
North Carolina State University offers cooperative education programs.

www.onlineschools.net
Monster's Learning Network includes a source to help you find the right school.

Job Services and Career Advice

http://career-advice.monster.com
Monster career information and job and internship listings.

http://orlandojobspot.blogspot.com
Job-hunting tips and employment opportunities.

www.us.manpower.com
Manpower, Inc. offers job search by locality and employment resources.

www.vault.com
VAULT, Career information and job and internship listings.

Money-Saving Ideas

www.ams.usda.gov/farmersmarkets
Find a local farmers market.

www.bigwords.com
Buy and sell textbooks online from student to student.

www.craigslist.com

A collection of online want ads that is available in many areas.

www.dentistry.umn.edu

University of Minnesota Dental Clinics offer low-cost dental care.

www.farmersmarket.com

Find a local farmers market.

www.freecycle.org

Check in your area for all kinds of free stuff.

www.thefrugallife.com

Information on how to live frugally with what you have.

www.half.ebay.com

Buy and sell textbooks online from student to student.

www.iCollegeWeb.com

Buy and sell textbooks online from student to student.

www.livingonadime.com

Newsletters and articles with money-saving tips.

www.MySavingPlace.com

Tips and advice on saving money.

www.textbookx.com

Buy and sell textbooks online from student to student.

www.venicefamilyclinic.org

Provides free healthcare to low-income patients who lack health insurance.

http://zenhabits.net/the-cheapskate-guide-50-tips-for-frugal-living
Zen Habits offers a forum to help you save on money by cutting back on expenses.

Organizational Ideas

www.cableorganizer.com
Items for your office or home.

www.lifeorganizers.com
Organizational tips and resources.

Scholarship, Grant, and Loan Information and Assistance

www.benefits.va.gov/gibill
Veteran's Administration provides educational benefits for vets.

www.bie.edu
Bureau of Indian Education offers educational benefits to eligible American Indian/Alaska Native students.

www.collegeboard.org
Contains information about College Board activities, including AP courses and CLEP exams.www.essayedge.com The world's largest application essay editing company.

https://fafsa.ed.gov
This site has the web-based version of the FAFSA application.

www.ftc.gov/scholarshipscams
A site regarding scholarship scams.

www.finaid.org/calculators
Worksheets for estimating EFC.

www.gocollege.com
A source of information for school funding.

www.grants.gov
The official United States government resource for prospective students offers a free, downloadable handbook to every federal student aid program.

www.hbsguru.com
The Cambridge Essay Service provides assistance with editing your essays.

www.instantcollegeadmissionessay.com
College Admission Essay Toolkit.

www.instantrecommendationletterkit.com
Recommendation letter kit; covers all types of recommendation letters and reference letters including those for college admission and jobs.

http://mappingyourfuture.org
Mapping Your Future is a public-service, nonprofit website providing career, college, financial aid, and financial literacy information and services.

http://oedb.org
The Online Education Database is a search engine that contains available college funding state-by-state.

www.suntrusteducation.com
SunTrust Bank offers student loans and savings programs.

https://studentaid.ed.gov/sa
The U.S. Department of Education's site.

www.studentclearinghouse.org
A clearinghouse designed to allow you to order all of your transcripts online.

Travel

www.amtrak.com
Official site for Amtrak passenger trains featuring online reservations, ticket fare finder, trip planning resources, and more.

www.expedia.com
Discount travel site.

www.orbitz.com
Discount travel site.

www.syta.org
The nonprofit, professional trade association that promotes student and youth travel and seeks to foster integrity and professionalism among student and youth travel service providers.

www.travelbyyen.com
Travel agency that also works with students for their travel needs.

www.travelocity.com
Discount travel site.

www.travelzoo.com
Discount travel site.

Work and Service Programs

www.bankofamerica.com
Bank of America offers student loan and savings programs.

www.nationalguard.com
The Reserves and the National Guard offer college benefits that you could be entitled to.

www.nationalservice.gov/programs/americorps
AmeriCorps provides work opportunities in communities across the country. Upon completion you can apply for a school scholarship.

Other

www.bbb.org
The Better Business Bureaus works to ensure that high standards for businesses are set and maintained.

www.coachphyllis.com
Life coaching and guidance.

www.susan-johnston.com
Freelance writer and blogger.

Glossary

The ACT: A standardized test produced by ACT, Inc. for college admissions in the United States.

The Advanced International Certificate of Education (AICE): An international curriculum that prepares students in the upper levels of high school for college and future employment.

Advanced Placement (AP): A program that places a high school student in a college-level course.

Bachelor's Degree: The academic degree that colleges or universities give students after studying for four years.

Board of Admissions: A committee that collectively determines whether or not an applicant is eligible to become a student at their university.

Community College: A junior college that offers courses to local students.

Community Service:
Non-paying, voluntary work that is performed for the benefit of society.

Commuter Student: A student who lives off-campus.

Doctorate: The highest academic degree that colleges and universities give students.

Dual Enrollment: When a student is enrolled in two or more academic institutions — generally, a high school student taking college courses.

Extracurricular Activities: Activities outside the scope of regular curricula (such as journalism, sports, or volunteer work).

Grade Point Average (GPA): The number that represents a student's average grade.

Graduate School: The part of a college or university that offers advanced academic programs for students who have already earned a bachelor's degree.

Grant: An amount of money given by an organization.

Guidance Counselor: A person employed by an academic institution to help students plan for the future.

Home-schooler: A student who is taught at home rather than in a public or private school.

International Baccalaureate (IB): An international educational foundation that offers educational programs for children between the ages of 3 and 19.

Internship: A temporary position that offers on-the-job training instead of employment.

Ivy League Schools: A group of eight renowned private colleges and universities in the Northeastern United States. The institutions are Brown University, Columbia University, Cornell University, Dartmouth College, Harvard University, the University of Pennsylvania, Princeton University, and Yale University.

Master's Degree: The academic degree that colleges or universities give students after one or two years of additional study after earning their bachelor's degree.

Residential Student: A student who lives on or near campus.

The SAT: A standardized test used in the United States for college admissions.

Scholarship: An amount of money awarded by an organization to support a student's education.

State College: A college that is financed by the state government.

Student Loan: Money leant at interest that is used to pay for a student's education.

Transcript: An official record that details the particulars of a student's work, including coursework and grades.

Undergraduate: A college or university student who has yet to earn a bachelor's degree.

Bibliography

AARP. 2008. **www.aarp.org/about_aarp/nrta/ed_associations**

The American Institute of Certified Public Accountants. 2007. **www.aicpa.org/InterestAreas/AccountingEducation/Pages/AEC.aspx**

Aaron, Susan. 2008. The Learning Coach. "Finish That Degree."

www.ama-assn.org. "Top 10 Things to Discuss with Your College Student Before Spring Break." Prepared by A Matter of Degree: The National Effort to Reduce High-Risk Drinking Among College Students. Content provided by: Alcohol & Drug Abuse. Mar 28, 2005.

www.associatedcontent.com. "What Should You Consider Before Dropping a College Course? Cutting Your Course Load Can Impact More Than Just Your GPA." M. Pam. Feb 21, 2007.

www.bcsalliance.com. "Budgeting: How to Reduce Monthly Expenses." **www.bcsalliance.com/budgeting-reduce-monthly-expenses.html**

www.bcbs.com. "Study Results Show Medical Expenses Reduced with Preventive Health Program." Egel, Valerie. December 5, 2007. **http://mediacenter.bcbsnc.com/news/59928**

Belluck, Pam. "Harvard, for Less: Extension Courses' New Allure" *The New York Times*, November 18, 2005. **www.nytimes.com/2005/11/18/national/18harvard.html?ei=5088&en=7812fb4a9883e35e&ex=1289970000&partner=rssnyt&emc=rss&pagewanted=all**

California Retired Teachers Association. 2008. **www.calrta.org**

Cardtrack.com. 2008. "Credit Card Debt — What Do Americans Really Owe?" Media Center.

www.census.gov. "Census Bureau Data Underscore Value of College Degree." Bergman, Mike. March 28, 2005.

College Board. 2007. **www.collegeboard.com**

College Compass. 2007. **www.edonline.com/collegecompass**

College Board's Trends in College Pricing 2007, Trends in Student Aid 2007, and Education Pays. 2007. **www.collegeboard.com/student/pay/add-it-up/4494.html**

DataMasters. **www.datamasters.com**

Federal Trade Commission. 2007. **www.ftc.gov/scholarshipscams**

Federal Trade Commission. "Searching for College Money?" September 5, 1996. **www.ftc.gov/news-events/press-releases/1996/09/searching-college-money**

FindAid. 2007. **www.finaid.org**

www.freecycle.org. 2007. "Mission Statement." **www.freecycle.org/about/missionstatement**

Huddleston, Cameron. "Everything You Need to Know About College Aid: Know the Sources, Learn the Process and Apply Early to Get Your Share of the College Funding Pot of Gold." Kiplinger.com, Feb. 6, 2007. **www.kiplinger.com/features/archives/2007/02/financialaid.html**

J.D. "16 Ways to Eat Healthy While Keeping It Cheap." July, 30 2007.

Julian, Tiffany. "Work-Life Earnings by Field of Degree and Occupation for People with a Bachelor's Degree: 2011." *U.S. Census Bureau* (2012). *United States Census Bureau*. Web. 29 Aug. 2016.

www.getrichslowly.org/blog/2007/07/30/16-ways-to-eat-healthy-while-keeping-it-cheap

Lazarony, Lucy. "Good Deeds Help Pay Down College Debt." Bankrate.com, May 4, 2004.

"Making Sense of Scholarships: The Ultimate Resource for Successfully Securing College Funding and Grants." 2006. **www.ecrater.com/product.php?pid=1553199**

Nellie Mae. A Sallie Mae Student Loan Company. 2007. **www.nelliemae.com/library/scholarships.html**

Nicole, Allen. Textbooks Advocate. "5 Ways to Save on Textbooks Now, 3 Ways to Lower Prices Long Term." August 22, 2007. **www.studentpirgs.org/news/5-ways-save-textbooks-now-3-ways-lower-prices-long-term**

O'Connor, Tricia, CPA. "How to Dig Yourself Out of Credit Card Debt." *Denver Business Journal.* 4 July, 1997. **www.bizjournals.com/denver/stories/1997/07/07/smallb4.html?page=2**

www.opportunitiesaplenty.com. 2007. "Why Consolidate Your Loans or Other Debt?"

Pew Research Center. "Are We Happy Yet?" **www.pewsocialtrends.org/2006/02/13/are-we-happy-yet**

Pew Research Center. "As Marriage and Parenthood Drift Apart, Public Is Concerned About Social Impact: Generation Gap in Values, Behaviors." July 1, 2007. **www.pewresearch.org/pubs/526/marriage-parenthood**

The Project on Student Debt. 2006. **www.projectonstudentdebt.org**

The San Diego Union-Tribune. "Starting Salaries for College Grads." February 20, 2006. **www.signonsandiego.com/uniontrib/20060220/news_lz1n20thelist.html**

Sanchez, Claudio. "Book Costs Shock College Students, Families." July 25, 2006. **www.npr.org/templates/story/story.php?storyId=5580358**

Singletary, Michelle. 2006. "Books: Colleges' Budget-Busters." Washingtonpost.com, July 13. **www.washingtonpost.com/wp-dyn/content/article/2006/07/12/AR2006071201979_pf.html**

Stony Brook University. Scholarships, Fellowships & Awards. 2007. **www.stonybrook.edu/commcms/finaid/typesofaid/scholarships.html**

Student Aid on the Web. "Loan Consolidation." June 22, 1007. **www.studentaid.ed.gov**

Student Aid on the Web. "Looking for Student Aid...Without Getting Scammed." Sept. 17, 2007. **www.studentaid.ed.gov/ PORTALSWebApp/students/english/lsa.jsp**

Student Youth Travel Association. "Free Travel Safety Tips Brochure." July 13, 2004. **www.syta.org/downloads/Safety%20Tips%20 Brochure2009.pdf**

SunTrust Bank. 2007. **http://moneyforcollege.suntrust.com**

U.S. Census Bureau. 2007. **www.census.gov**

U.S. Department of Education. 2007. U.S. Department of Education. **www.ed.gov**

U.S. Department of Education. 2007. "Loan Consolidation." **www.ed.gov/offices/OSFAP/DCS/consolidation.html**

The Vegetarian Resource Group. 2007. **www.vrg.org/student/scholar.htm**

Weston, Liz Pulliam. 2007. "The Basics: How to Find Free Money for College." MSN Money.

Wikipedia. "Scholarship." December 19, 2007. **https://en.wikipedia.org/wiki/Scholarship**

Wikipedia. "Stafford Loan." December 5, 2007. **https://en.wikipedia.org/wiki/Stafford_loan**

Witkop, Lori. "Minority Scholarships." 28 June 2006. **http://college.lovetoknow.com/Minority_Scholarships**

www.yale.edu. Adapted from a handout provided by Jane Curlin, Willamette University. "How to Ask for — and Get — Strong Letters of Recommendation." October 9, 2007.

Index

About the Authors

Ann Marie O'Phelan, M.F.A.

Ann has a B.A. degree in Advertising and Business Management from Metropolitan State University, Minneapolis, and an M.F.A degree in Creative Writing from National University, San Diego, where she graduated with Distinction. She worked full-time through all of her schooling, and received merit-based scholarships, and scholarships that were available through local organizations — all helping to reduce her student loans.

Her writing background includes working as an advertising copywriter for notable advertising agencies in Minneapolis, Chicago, and Los Angeles, where she won national and international awards for her work. She currently writes for numerous newspapers and publications, and teaches online writing courses for several universities.

"Pleasure in the job puts perfection in the work."
Aristotle (384 BC - 322 BC)

Debra Lipphardt

I am a proud grandmother (aka "Nonnie") of my beautiful granddaughter Aubrey, a just as proud mother of Jessica and Michael, and a wife. Career wise, I am the Career and College Center Specialist and Scholarship Coordinator for a local high school in our county. I actually added on the position of Scholarship Coordinator myself, because I found the results of winning scholarships so fascinating and rewarding for my students, and much of my scholarship work is done during my own time at home.

Our students have won the most awards for the past 15 out of 16 years over the other six schools in our district since I began working with scholarships, averaging over $6 million yearly for the past five years, and I have given countless lectures and workshops, weekly private meetings with parents and students, and have been interviewed on several local and national radio stations. Some of my awards received for my work with scholarships include the County School Employee of the Year in 2000 and 2004, as well as District Teacher of the Year for the VFW several times (even though I am not a teacher), and multiple nominations for several Who's Who organizations for professionals and business leaders.

Besides my family, scholarships and helping students are my passions in life, and both are something I will continue to do, even after retirement.